中国职业教育"汉语+"系列

《旅游汉语》编委会

主　编　芦　妍　吴安萍　张　琼

编　委　韩淑靖　王抒诣　郭　嫣　董鸿安

　　　　何　越　林　超　沈永军　程　帅

中国职业教育"汉语+"系列

总主编 岑 咏 吴安萍

旅游汉语
LÜYOU HANYU

主编 芦 妍 吴安萍 张 琼

ZHEJIANG UNIVERSITY PRESS
浙江大学出版社
·杭州·

图书在版编目（CIP）数据

　　旅游汉语 / 芦妍，吴安萍，张琼主编. -- 杭州 ：
浙江大学出版社，2025. 5. --（中国职业教育"汉语+
"系列 / 岑咏，吴安萍总主编）. -- ISBN 978-7-308
-25696-4

　　Ⅰ. H195.4

　　中国国家版本馆CIP数据核字第20257TX199号

旅游汉语

芦　妍　吴安萍　张　琼　主编

丛书策划	黄静芬
责任编辑	杨诗怡
责任校对	仝　林
封面设计	林智广告
出版发行	浙江大学出版社
	（杭州市天目山路148号　邮政编码310007）
	（网址：http://www.zjupress.com）
排　　版	杭州林智广告有限公司
印　　刷	杭州宏雅印刷有限公司
开　　本	787mm×1092mm　1/16
印　　张	12.75
字　　数	242千
版印次	2025年5月第1版　2025年5月第1次印刷
书　　号	ISBN 978-7-308-25696-4
定　　价	68.00元

PREFACE 前言

　　在全球化的今天，旅游已经成为人们生活中不可或缺的一部分。随着中国的快速发展和国际化进程的推进，越来越多的外国游客选择中国作为他们的旅行目的地。为了更好地理解和融入中国的文化和生活，学习汉语成为了一项重要的需求。中国职业教育"汉语+"系列的《旅游汉语》应运而生，本书旨在为广大来华旅游爱好者和实用汉语学习者提供实际有效的学习工具，帮助他们更好地掌握与旅游相关的汉语语言技能。

　　本书以实用为导向，内容涵盖了常见的旅游场景，从酒店入住、餐厅点餐到交通出行等各个场景。依据党的二十大报告中提出的"坚持以文塑旅、以旅彰文，推进文化和旅游深度融合发展"[1]的理念，本教材特别融入了中国的历史、文化、社会和自然元素。通过生动的对话和情景模拟，学习者可以在短时间内掌握基本的沟通技巧，能够在实际交流场合中使用汉语自信应对各种情况，从而提升旅行体验。

　　本书不仅仅是一部语言教材，它还注重与旅游相关的中国文化的介绍和社会习俗的传授。通过对中国传统习俗和现代社会的了解，读者可以更加深入地体验和欣赏中国的丰富多彩。因此，在本书的学习过程中，学习者不仅能够获得语言能力的提升，更能够感受到中国文化交流的魅力；不仅能够在旅途中游刃有余，更能通过语言的桥梁，深入体验和了解中国的历史和现代发展，更好地融入和理解中国，从而增强中华文明传播力影响力，深化文明交流互鉴，推动中华文化更好走向世界。

1　习近平：高举中国特色社会主义伟大旗帜 为全面建设社会主义现代化国家而团结奋斗——在中国共产党第二十次全国代表大会上的报告 .（2022-10-25）[2024-09-25].https://www.gov.cn/xinwen/2022/10/25/content_5721685.htm.

中国式现代化是全体人民共同富裕的现代化，强调的是全体人民共同富裕、物质文明和精神文明相协调、人与自然和谐共生。这一理念为我们的旅游汉语教材提供了深刻的文化内涵和实践指导。因此，在编写本教材的过程中，编者积极开展与希尔顿连锁酒店集团、浙江达人旅业股份有限公司、浙江飞扬国际旅游集团的合作，校企协同，共同涉及了注重真实性、创新性、实用性的教学内容。我们的目标是让学习者在学习汉语的同时，也能够体验到中国式现代化的独特魅力。[1]

作为中国职业教育"汉语+"系列的教材之一，本教材得到了宁波职业技术学院校党委、国合处、国际商旅学院的大力支持，在此表示衷心的感谢。

由于时间和篇幅所限，书中难免有疏漏之处，恳请广大读者批评指正。

1　习近平：高举中国特色社会主义伟大旗帜 为全面建设社会主义现代化国家而团结奋斗——在中国共产党第二十次全国代表大会上的报告.（2022-10-25）[2024-09-25].https://www.gov.cn/xinwen/2022-10/25/content_5721685.htm.

汉语词类简称 Abbreviations

动词（动）	dòngcí	verb (v.)
名词（名）	míngcí	noun (n.)
代词（代）	dàicí	pronoun (pron.)
形容词（形）	xíngróngcí	adjective (adj.)
副词（副）	fùcí	adverb (adv.)
介词（介）	jiècí	preposition (prep.)
数词（数）	shùcí	numeral (num.)
量词（量）	liàngcí	measure word (m.)
连词（连）	liáncí	conjunction (conj.)
叹词（叹）	tàncí	interjection (interj.)
助词（助）	zhùcí	particle (part.)

《旅游汉语》人物表 Characters

张老师（女，中国）

沙地（男，叙利亚）

CONTENTS 目录

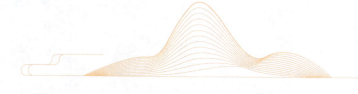

第一单元

机场

Unit 1
Airport

在本单元，你将要学习在中国的机场的常用词汇和交际用语，这些表达能够帮助你顺利地完成出入境、行李托运、安全检查等过程。同时，本单元还将介绍中国的机场的特点和文化，你将更好地了解机场这一场景。

In this unit, you will learn some commonly-used words and communication phrases used at Chinese airports, which will help you smoothly complete processes such as entry and exit, baggage check-in, and security check. Additionally, this unit will also introduce the characteristics and culture of Chinese airports, allowing you to better understand the airport scenes in China.

登机
Check in

**课前热身 Warm up**

1. 你在机场遇到过什么问题吗？
2. 机场里有哪些指示牌呢？

课文 Texts

课文一

A：我想买一张去上海的机票。

B：您想买单程机票还是往返机票？

A：往返机票。

B：哪天的？请问是哪天出发？

A：明天出发，下周二回来。

B：您想要经济舱还是商务舱？

A：经济舱。

B：这是您的机票。

A：好的，谢谢。

kèwén yī

A：Wǒ xiǎng mǎi yì zhāng qù Shànghǎi de jīpiào.

B：Nín xiǎng mǎi dānchéng jīpiào háishi wǎngfǎn jīpiào?

A：Wǎngfǎn jīpiào.

B：Nǎ tiān de? Qǐngwèn shì nǎ tiān chūfā?

A：Míngtiān chūfā, xià zhōuèr huílái.

B：Nín xiǎngyào jīngjì cāng háishi shāngwù cāng?

A：Jīngjì cāng.

B：Zhè shì nín de jīpiào.

A：Hǎo de, xièxie.

课内练习 Exercises

一　**分角色朗读课文**。Role-play the conversation.

二　**根据课文内容，回答问题**。Answer questions according to the text.

1. A要去哪儿?

2. A想哪天出发?

3. A想要经济舱还是商务舱?

三　**听一听，跟读句子**。Listen and read the sentences.

1. 我想买一张去上海的机票。

2. 您想买单程机票还是往返机票?

3. 请问是哪天出发?

4. 您想要经济舱还是商务舱?

5. 这是您的机票。

生词学习 New words

我（代）	wǒ	I, me
想（动）	xiǎng	want to do
买（动）	mǎi	buy
张（量）	zhāng	a measure word for tickets
机票（名）	jīpiào	air ticket
单程（形）	dānchéng	single-way
往返（形）	wǎngfǎn	round-trip
还是（副）	háishi	or
哪（代）	nǎ	which
明天（名）	míngtiān	tomorrow
下（副）	xià	next (for time)
经济舱（名）	jīngjì cāng	economy class
商务舱（名）	shāngwù cāng	business class
这（代）	zhè	this
谢谢（动）	xièxie	thanks

课文 Texts

课文二

A：请问去上海的飞机是在这里值机吗？

B：是的。您想要什么样的座位，靠窗的还是靠过道的？

A：靠窗的。

B：好的，您有行李需要托运吗？

A：有的。这是我的行李箱。

B：好的。行李没有问题，这是您的登机牌
和行李托运小票，您可以去安检了。

A：谢谢。

kèwén èr

A：Qǐngwèn qù Shànghǎi de fēijī shì zài zhèlǐ zhíjī ma?

B：Shì de. Nín xiǎng yào shénmeyàng de zuòwèi,
kào chuāng de háishi kào guòdào de?

A：Kào chuāng de.

B：Hǎo de, nín yǒu xíngli xūyào tuōyùn ma?

A：Yǒu de. Zhè shì wǒ de xíngli xiāng.

B：Hǎo de. Xíngli méiyǒu wèntí, zhè shì nín de dēngjī pái hé xíngli tuōyùn
xiǎopiào, nín kěyǐ qù ānjiǎn le.

A：Xièxie.

课内练习 Exercises

一 **分角色朗读课文。** Role-play the conversation.

二 **根据课文内容，回答问题。** Answer questions according to the text.

1. A想要什么样的座位？

2. A有行李需要托运吗？

3. A下一步去做什么？

三 **听一听，跟读句子**。Listen and read the sentences.

1. 请问去上海的飞机是在这里值机吗？
2. 您想要什么样的座位？
3. 靠窗的还是靠过道的？
4. 您有行李需要托运吗？
5. 这是您的登机牌和行李托运小票。

生词学习　New words

去（动）	qù	go
上海（名）	Shànghǎi	shanghai
飞机（名）	fēijī	plane
值机（动）	zhíjī	check in
这里（代）	zhèlǐ	here
什么样（代）	shénmeyàng	what kind of
座位（名）	zuòwèi	seat
靠（动）	kào	lean on
过道（名）	guòdào	aisle
窗户（名）	chuānghu	window
行李（名）	xíngli	luggage
托运（动）	tuōyùn	consignment
有（动）	yǒu	have
没有（副）	méiyǒu	not
问题（名）	wèntí	problem
登机牌（名）	dēngjī pái	boarding pass
小票（名）	xiǎopiào	ticket
安检（名）	ānjiǎn	security check

言点链接 Language points

一 陈述句的用法 Usage of 陈述句（chénshù jù）

陈述句是汉语语法中一种最基本的句式类型，通常用来表达陈述、叙述或说明某种事实、情况或观点。在陈述句中，主语一般在句首，谓语在主语之后，而补语则可以出现在句子的任何位置。陈述句可以通过调整语序来表达不同的语言习惯或语境，但其核心结构始终由主语、谓语和补语构成。此外，陈述句还可以通过语气的变化来表达不同的情感或意图。例如，陈述语气用于表达客观的事实，疑问语气用于提问，祈使语气用于请求或命令。

The declarative sentence is one of the most basic sentence types in Chinese grammar, which is usually used to express a statement, narration, or explanation of certain facts, situations, or viewpoints. In a declarative sentence, the subject generally appears at the beginning of the sentence, followed by the predicate, and the complement can appear in any position of the sentence. The word order of declarative sentences can be adjusted to express different language habits or contexts, but the core structure always consists of subject, predicate, and complement. In addition, the mood of declarative sentences can be changed to express different emotions or intentions. For example, declarative mood is used to express objective facts, interrogative mood is used to ask questions, and imperative mood is used to make requests or commands.

（1）我是中国人。

（2）我想去上海。

（3）他们是我的同学。

（4）她买了一瓶水。

（5）下个学期给我们上课的老师是张老师。

二 时间词的用法 Usage of 时间词（shíjiān cí）

时间词是指用于表示时间的单词或短语，包括基本时间词（如年、月、日、时、分、秒等）和表示时间段或时间点的词语（如今天、明天、昨天、上午、下午、晚上、星期、月份、季节等）。时间词在语言中发挥了重要的作用，可以帮助人们描述事件发生的顺序、时刻、频率、持续时间等方面的信息。在语法上，时间词可以作为时间状语或时间主语出现，用于修饰动词或构成句子的主语。此外，时间词的语义也受到文化、习惯和语言环境等方面的影响，不同的语言和文化传统对于时间的理解和表达方式也会存在差异。

Time words refer to words or phrases used to indicate time, including basic time words (such as year, month, day, hour, minute, second, etc.) and words that indicate time periods or points in time (such as today, tomorrow, yesterday, morning, afternoon, evening, week, month, season, etc.). Time words play an important role in language, helping people describe the sequence, moments, frequency, and duration of events. Grammatically, time words can be used as time adverbs or time subjects, modifying verbs or serving as the subject of a sentence. In addition, the semantics of time words are also influenced by cultural, customary, and linguistic factors. Different languages and cultural traditions may have differences in understanding and expressing time.

Common time words include:

昨天	上周 / 上个星期	上个月	去年
今天	这周 / 这个星期	这个月	今年
明天	下周 / 下个星期	下个月	明年

---

❶ 注意NOTE：

"上个星期"和"下个星期"中的"上"和"下"是汉语中的时间词，表示时间的顺序关系。其中，"上"表示在当前时间之前的时间，即过去的时间；而"下"表示在当前时间之后的时间，即未来的时间。因此，"上个星期"表示的是过去一个星期，即上星期；而"下个星期"表示的是未来一个星期，即下星期。这种使用"上"和"下"表示时间顺序的方式在汉语中非常常见，例如，"上个月""下个月""上午""下午"等。需要注意的是，"上"和"下"在不同的语境中也可以表示其他含义，需要根据具体语境进行理解。

The "上" and "下" in "上个星期" and "下个星期" are time words in Chinese that indicate the order of time. The word "上" indicates a time that is before the current time, i.e., the past; while "下" indicates a time that is after the current time, i.e., the future. Therefore, "上个星期" means last week, which refers to the past week; while "下个星期" means next week, which refers to the coming week. This way of expressing time order using "上" and "下" is very common in Chinese, such as "上个月" (last month), "下个月" (next month), "上午" (morning), "下午" (afternoon). It should be noted that "上" and "下" can also have other meanings in different contexts, and their meanings should be understood based on the specific context.

三 "还是"的用法 Usage of "还是（háishi）"

"还是"在汉语语法中是表示选择疑问句的从句连词，用于引导一个陈述句和一个疑问句，表示在两个或多个选项之间做出选择的关系。当"还是"连接两个并列的选项时，句子的语序通常为"是A还是B"。在这种语法结构中，通常第一个选项为肯定句，第二个选项为疑问句。例如，"你是喝茶还是咖啡？"中的"还是"就用来表示在喝茶和喝咖啡两个选项之间做出选择的关系。在汉语中使用"还是"还有其他语法意思，如对比、强调、比较等。根据上下文和交际目的合理使用"还是"十分重要，否则可能会影响句子的表达和理解。

"还是" in Chinese grammar is a subordinate conjunction used to introduce a selection question sentence, indicating a choice between two or more options. When "还是" connects two parallel options, the sentence structure is usually "是 A 还是 B". In this grammar structure, the first option is usually an affirmative sentence, and the second option is an interrogative sentence. For example, in the sentence "你是喝茶还是咖啡？" (Do you drink tea or coffee?), "还是" is used to indicate a choice between two options, drinking tea or coffee. The use of "还是" in Chinese language also has other grammatical meanings such as contrast, emphasis, comparison, etc. It is important to use "还是" appropriately according to the context and communicative purpose, otherwise it may affect the expression and understanding of the sentence. For example:

（1）您想买单程机票还是往返机票？

（2）您想要经济舱还是商务舱？

（3）您想要靠窗的还是靠过道的？

（4）你想喝苹果汁还是橙汁？

四 "想"的用法 Usage of "想（xiǎng）"

"想"是一个汉语常用词，具有多种用法。以下是常见的几种：

（1）表示思考、思索的意思，如："我正在想这个问题该如何解决。"

（2）表示心理上的愿望、意愿，如："我想吃饭了。""我想去旅游。"

（3）表示推测、猜测的意思，如："我想他应该已经到家了。"

（4）表示做某事的打算或意图，如："我想明天去图书馆看书。"

（5）表示询问或请求，如："你想不想喝杯茶？""我想请你帮我一个忙。"

（6）与"要""需要"等动词连用，表示需要或必须的意思。

"想" is a commonly used word in Chinese with multiple uses. Here are some of the common usages:

（1）To express thinking or pondering, as in "I am thinking about how to solve this problem."

（2）To indicate a psychological desire or wish, such as "I want to eat now." or "I want to travel."

（3）To suggest guessing or speculation, as in "I think he must have arrived home by now."

（4）To express the intention or plan to do something, as in "I plan to go to the library to read books tomorrow."

（5）To express inquiry or request, such as "Would you like to have a cup of tea?" or "I would like to ask you for a favor."

（6）When used in conjunction with verbs such as "要" or "需要", it conveys a sense of need or necessity.

课后练习 Exercises

一 看拼音写汉字。Look at the pinyin and write the words.

zhí jī	ān jiǎn	guò dào	xiǎng	jī piào
（　　）	（　　）	（　　）	（　　）	（　　）

hái shi	chū fā	dān chéng	jīng jì cāng	xíng li
（　　）	（　　）	（　　）	（　　）	（　　）

二 选词填空。Choose the correct words to fill in the blanks.

上海	值机	还是	经济舱	想要

1. 我（　　）喝咖啡。

2. 请问是在这里（　　）吗？

3. 请问你买（　　）还是商务舱？

4. 这张机票是去（　　）的。

5. 你想这周（　　）下周去拜访别的公司？

三 把下面的词语整理成句子。Rearrange the following words and phrases to make sentences.

1. 想要　　你　　面包　　还是　　牛奶

2. 哪天　　请问　　我们　　出发

3. 她　　买　　电影票　　一张　　想

4. 这　　你的　　行李箱　　吗　　是

5. 上海　　去　　下周　　我们

四 回答问题。Answer the questions.

1. 你喜欢靠窗的还是靠过道的座位？

_____

2. 你想买去哪儿的机票？

_____

3. 我们先值机还是先安检？

_____

4. 你明天想做什么？

_____

5. 公司一般会买什么舱位的机票？

_____

五 听录音，判断对错。Listen to the recording and judge whether the statements are correct or incorrect.

1. 她想买去上海的机票。　　☐

2. 今天没有机票了。　　☐

3. 她想买两张经济舱。　　☐

4. 她想买靠窗的机票。　　☐

5. 她今天下午一点到机场值机。　　☐

机上服务

In-Flight Service

 前热身 **Warm up**

1. 你对飞机上的什么美食有印象？
2. 你对飞机上的哪些服务比较满意？

课文 **Texts**

课文一

A：欢迎乘坐本次航班。

请您系好安全带，我们的飞机马上就要起飞了。

您好，有什么可以帮助您的吗？

B：我有点儿冷。可以给我一条毯子吗？

A：好的，先生。我先帮您调小空调。

B：谢谢。

A：先生，这是您要的毯子。

B：谢谢。

kèwén yī

A：Huānyíng chéngzuò běn cì hángbān.

Qǐng nín jì hǎo ānquándài, wǒmen de fēijī mǎshàng jiù yào qǐfēi le.

Nín hǎo, yǒu shénme kěyǐ bāngzhù nín de ma?

B：Wǒ yǒudiǎnr lěng. Kěyǐ gěi wǒ yì tiáo tǎnzi ma?

A：Hǎo de, xiānsheng. Wǒ xiān bāng nín tiáo xiǎo kōngtiáo.

B：Xièxie.

A：Xiānsheng, zhè shì nín yào de tǎnzi.

B：Xièxie.

课内练习 Exercises

一　分角色朗读课文。Role-play the conversation.

二　根据课文内容，回答问题。Answer questions according to the text.

1. 乘客觉得怎么样？

2. 乘客想要什么？

3. 乘务员先进行什么处理？

三　听一听，跟读句子。Listen and read the sentences.

1. 欢迎乘坐本次航班。

2. 请您系好安全带，我们的飞机马上就要起飞了。

3. 您好，有什么可以帮助您的吗？

4. 可以给我一条毯子吗？

5. 我先帮您调小空调。

生词学习 New words

欢迎（动）	huānyíng	welcome
乘坐（动）	chéngzuò	ride
本（代）	běn	this
次（量）	cì	time
航班（名）	hángbān	flight
系（动）	jì	tie
安全带（名）	ānquándài	seat belt
马上（副）	mǎshàng	right away
起飞（动）	qǐfēi	take off
帮助（动）	bāngzhù	help
冷（形）	lěng	cold
给（动）	gěi	give
毯子（名）	tǎnzi	blanket
帮（动）	bāng	help
调（动）	tiáo	adjust
空调（名）	kōngtiáo	air conditioner

 **Texts**

课文二

A：先生，您好。请问您要喝点什么吗？

B：有什么喝的呢？

A：我们有苹果汁、橙汁、菠萝汁、咖啡、茶和水。

B：请给我一杯苹果汁。

A：好的，先生。这是我们提供的机餐，祝您用餐愉快。

B：谢谢。

（降落前）

A：各位乘客，我们的飞机即将降落，
　　请您调直椅背，打开遮光板，系好安全带。
　　谢谢您的配合。

kèwén èr

A：Xiānsheng, nínhǎo.

　　Qǐngwèn nín yào hē diǎn shénme ma?

B：Yǒu shénme hē de ne?

A：Wǒmen yǒu píngguǒ zhī、chéngzhī、bōluó zhī、kāfēi、chá hé shuǐ.

B：Qǐng gěi wǒ yì bēi píngguǒ zhī.

A：Hǎo de, xiānsheng. Zhè shì wǒmen tígōng de jīcān, zhù nín yòngcān yúkuài.

B：Xièxie.

（jiàngluò qián）

A：Gèwèi chéngkè, wǒmen de fēijī jíjiāng jiàngluò, qǐng nín tiáo zhí yǐbèi,

　　dǎkāi zhē guāng bǎn, jì hǎo ānquándài. Xièxie nín de pèihé.

内练习 **Exercises**

一　分角色朗读课文。Role-play the conversation.

二　根据课文内容，回答问题。Answer questions according to the text.

1. 飞机上有什么喝的？

2. B想喝什么？

3. 飞机降落的时候要做些什么？

三 **听一听，跟读句子**。Listen and read the sentences.

1. 请问您要喝点什么吗？

2. 我们有苹果汁、橙汁、菠萝汁、咖啡、茶和水。

3. 这是我们提供的机餐，祝您用餐愉快。

4. 我们的飞机即将降落，请您调直椅背，打开遮光板，系好安全带。

5. 谢谢您的配合。

生词学习 New words

先生（名）	xiānsheng	sir
喝（动）	hē	drink
苹果汁（名）	píngguǒ zhī	apple juice
菠萝汁（名）	bōluó zhī	pineapple juice
橙汁（名）	chéng zhī	orange juice
咖啡（名）	kāfēi	coffee
茶（名）	chá	tea
机餐（名）	jīcān	in-flight meal
提供（动）	tígōng	provide
即将（副）	jíjiāng	soon
降落（动）	jiàngluò	land
直（形）	zhí	straight
椅背（名）	yǐbèi	back of the chair
打开（动）	dǎkāi	open
遮光板（名）	zhē guāng bǎn	visor
配合（名）	pèihé	cooperation

语言点链接 Language points

一 "要……了"的用法 Usage of "要（yào）……了（le）"

"要……了"是一个表示即将发生某种情况或某种动作的汉语语法结构，通常表示将要发生的动作或情况比较紧急或重要。其中，"要"表示将要发生的动作或情况，"了"则表示动作或情况已经完成或即将完成。这个结构中的"要"通常伴随一定的语气助词，如"快要""马上要"，以强调即将发生的动作或情况的紧迫性。这个语法结构常用于表示未来将要发生的动作或情况，且一般比较肯定。

"要……了" is a Chinese grammatical structure that indicates an imminent action or situation, often representing an urgent or important event that is about to happen. "要" indicates the action or situation that is going to happen, while "了" implies the completion or near-completion of the action or situation. The "要" in this structure is often accompanied by a certain modal particle, such as "快要" or "马上要", to emphasize the urgency of the action or situation that is about to happen. This grammatical structure is commonly used to indicate a future event that is likely to happen, and is generally affirmative.

（1）飞机马上要起飞了。

（2）飞机马上要降落了。

（3）我们要放假了。

（4）天快要下雨了。

二 结果补语的用法 Usage of 结果补语（jiéguǒ bǔyǔ）

结果补语是用来表示动作或状态的结果的语言成分，通常由形容词、副词、动词等词类构成，主要位于动词或形容词的后面，用来补充说明或强调动作或状态的结果。汉语中，结果补语通常不与"得"连用，例如："吃饱了""高兴极了""变化大了"等。

其中，形容词是表示状态或特征的词语，可以作为结果补语来表示状态或动作的结果，如"长大了""兴奋极了""丰富多彩了"等。

除了形容词，动词也可以作为结果补语，如"打开了""关上了"等。在这些情况下，动词被用来表示动作的结果，例如："打开了门"中的"打开了"表示门已经被打开了。

Result complement is a linguistic element used to indicate the result of an action or state. It is usually composed of adjectives, adverbs, verbs, and other parts of speech and is placed after the verb or adjective to supplement and emphasize the result of the action or state. In Chinese, result complements usually do not connect with 得, for example, "吃饱了""高兴极了""变化大了".

Adjectives are words that express a state or feature and can be used as result complements to indicate the result of an action or state, such as "长大了""兴奋极了""丰富多彩了".

In addition to adjectives, verbs can also serve as result complements, such as "打开了""关上了". In these cases, verbs are used to indicate the result of an action, for example, "打开了" in "打开了门" indicates that the door has been opened.

（1）我帮您调小音量。

（2）请您调直椅背。

（3）这瓶可乐已经打开了。

（4）她学会了网上订票。

三 "的"字的用法 Usage of "的（de）"

"的"字结构是短语的结构类别之一，也称"'的'字短语"，指助词"的"附着于词或词组之后形成的具有名词功能的组合，常用作主语和宾语。它可以构成独立的名词性短语，如"红色的""美丽的"等，表示一种特定的属性或状态。

The "的" phrase structure is one of the phrase structure categories in Chinese. It is also known as the "的" phrase. It refers to a combination that has a noun function formed by the particle "的" attached after a word or phrase, which is commonly used as a subject or object. It can also form an independent noun phrase, such as "红色的" and "美丽的", representing a specific attribute or state.

四 "帮"和"帮助"的用法 Usage of "帮（bāng）" and "帮助（bāngzhù）"

"帮"和"帮助"都表示帮助别人的意思，但在使用上有一定的区别。"帮"通常作为一个动词，表示"帮忙，协助"，强调的是行动的过程，常用于口语中。例如："我可以帮你拿书。""他来帮我们打扫卫生了。"

"帮助"则常作为一个名词或动词，表示"援助，支持"，强调的是帮助具体的对象，也常用于正式场合或书面语中。例如："他需要我们的帮助。""我们应该相互帮助。"

"帮" and "帮助" both mean to help others, but there are some differences in usage.

"帮" is usually used as a verb, meaning "help, assist"and emphasizes the process of action, often used in spoken language. For example, "I can help you carry your books."or "He helped us clean the bathroom."

"帮助" is often used as a noun or a verb, meaning "aid, support", emphasizing the specific object being helped, and often used in formal occasions or written language. For example, "He needs our help."or "We should help each other.".

课后练习 Exercises

一 看拼音写汉字。Look at the pinyin and write the words.

huān yíng　　háng bān　　qǐ fēi　　kōng tiáo　　tǎn zi
（　　）　　（　　）　　（　　）　　（　　）　　（　　）

tí gōng　　jí jiāng　　jiàng luò　　tiáo zhí　　pèi hé
（　　）　　（　　）　　（　　）　　（　　）　　（　　）

二 选词填空。Choose the correct word to fill in the blanks.

| 帮 | 咖啡 | 配合 | 给 | 起飞 |

1. 请（　　）我一杯苹果汁。

2. 您想要喝（　　）还是茶？

3. 您可以（　　）我调直椅背吗？

4. 请您（　　）我们的安检。

5. 我们的飞机还有半个小时就要（　　）了。

三 把下面的词语整理成句子。Rearrange the following words and phrases to make sentences.

1. 她　放假　了　要

2. 他　搬家　我　帮

3. 您　系好　请　安全带

4. 用餐　祝　愉快　您

5. 即将　我们　飞机　的　降落

四 **回答问题**。Answer the questions.

1. 飞机上有哪些喝的？

_____

2. 飞机起飞和降落的时候要系好安全带吗？

_____

3. 什么情况下飞机上会提供机餐？

_____

4. 如果在飞机上觉得冷，可以怎么办？

_____

5. 飞机降落的时候要做些什么？

_____

五 **听录音，判断对错**。Listen to the recording and judge whether the statements are correct or incorrect.

1. 飞机将在一个小时后起飞。　　☐

2. 乘客已经调直椅背。　　☐

3. 乘客有点儿冷。　　☐

4. 乘客想喝咖啡。　　☐

5. 乘客想吃牛肉饭。　　☐

出 境

Exit

 前热身 **Warm up**

1. 出入境的时候需要准备哪些证件?

2. 出入境通常有哪些原因?

课 文 **Texts**

课文一

A：您好，请出示您的有效证件。

B：您好，这是我的护照。

A：谢谢，请您摘下帽子。感谢您的配合。
　请问您来中国做什么?

B：我来学习汉语。

A：您打算在中国待多长时间?

B：一年。

A：好的，祝您学习顺利。

kèwén yī

A：Nínhǎo, qǐng chūshì nín de yǒuxiào zhèngjiàn.

B：Nínhǎo, zhè shì wǒ de hùzhào.

A：Xièxie, qǐng nín zhāixià màozi. Gǎnxiè nín de pèihé.
　Qǐngwèn nín lái Zhōngguó zuò shénme?

B：Wǒ lái xuéxí hànyǔ.

A：Nín dǎsuàn zài Zhōngguó dāi duō cháng shíjiān?

B：Yì nián.

A：Hǎo de, zhù nín xuéxí shùnlì.

课内练习 Exercises

一 **分角色朗读课文**。Role-play the conversation.

二 **根据课文内容，回答问题**。Answer questions according to the text.

　　1. B的有效证件是什么？

　　2. B来中国做什么？

　　3. B打算在中国待多长时间？

三 **听一听，跟读句子**。Listen and read the sentences.

　　1. 请出示您的有效证件。

　　2. 这是我的护照。

　　3. 感谢您的配合。

　　4. 我来学习汉语。

　　5. 祝您学习顺利。

生词学习 New words

出示（动）	chūshì	show
有效（形）	yǒuxiào	valid
证件（名）	zhèngjiàn	document
护照（名）	hùzhào	passport
摘（动）	zhāi	take off
帽子（名）	màozi	hat
打算（动）	dǎsuàn	plan
待（动）	dāi	stay
多长	duō cháng	how long
祝（动）	zhù	wish
学习（动）	xuéxí	learn, study
顺利（形）	shùnlì	successful

 课文 Texts

课文二

A：喂，您好。请问是张老师吗？

B：是的，是沙地吗？

A：是我，老师，我已经通过海关了。
现在在等我的行李。

B：好的，我在出口处等你，不要着急。

A：谢谢老师。
老师，谢谢您来机场接我。麻烦您了。

B：别客气。一路辛苦了。
机场交通很方便，我们可以坐地铁到学校。

A：太好了，我们出发吧。

kèwén èr

A：Wèi, nín hǎo. Qǐngwèn shì Zhāng lǎoshī ma?

B：Shì de, shì Shādì ma?

A：Shì wǒ, lǎoshī, wǒ yǐjīng tōngguò hǎiguān le.
Xiànzài zài děng wǒ de xíngli.

B：Hǎo de, wǒ zài chūkǒu chù děng nǐ, búyào zháojí.

A：Xièxie lǎoshī.
Lǎoshī, Xièxie nín lái jīchǎng jiē wǒ. Máfan nín le.

B：Bié kèqi. Yí lù xīnkǔ le.
Jīchǎng jiāotōng hěn fāngbiàn, wǒmen kěyǐ zuò dìtiě dào xuéxiào.

A：Tài hǎo le, wǒmen chūfā ba.

课内练习 Exercises

一　**分角色朗读课文**。Role-play the conversation.

二　**根据课文内容，回答问题**。Answer questions according to the text.

　　1. A在等什么？

2. 老师在什么地方等学生？

3. 他们怎么去学校？

三 **听一听，跟读句子**。Listen and read the sentences.

1. 请问是张老师吗？

2. 我已经通过海关了。

3. 我在出口处等你。

4. 一路辛苦了。

5. 机场交通很方便，我们可以坐地铁到学校。

生词学习 New words

喂（叹）	wèi	hello through phone
老师（名）	lǎoshī	teacher
通过（动）	tōngguò	pass
海关（名）	hǎiguān	customs
等（动）	děng	wait
出口（名）	chūkǒu	exit
着急（形）	zháojí	hurry
接（动）	jiē	pick up
辛苦（形）	xīnkǔ	tiring
交通（名）	jiāotōng	traffic
方便（形）	fāngbiàn	convenient
地铁（名）	dìtiě	subway
出发（动）	chūfā	set out

语言点链接 Language points

一 **形容词谓语句的用法** Usage of 形容词谓语句（xíngróngcí wèiyǔ jù）

汉语中形容词谓语句是一种以形容词作为谓语的简单句，用于表示主语的性质、状态或特征等。

In Chinese, the adjective predicate sentence is a kind of simple sentence with adjective as predicate, which is used to express the nature, state or feature of the subject.

（1）你好。

（2）一路辛苦了。

（3）这个苹果汁很甜。

（4）她还没通过海关，她很着急。

二 "太……了"的用法 Usage of "太（tài）……了（le）"

"太……了"是一个常用的固定搭配，用来表示事物的程度非常之高，意思相当于"非常……""极其……""十分……"等，常用于口语和书面语中。

"太……了"通常由"太"和一个形容词或副词构成，形成一个独立的句子，或是作为主语、宾语、定语或状语等成分出现在句子中。

"太……了"可以用来形容各种事物的程度，用法简单、灵活，描绘出了一种强烈的感受，但在使用时需要注意语境和语气，避免表达过于夸张或过于生硬。

"太……了" is a common fixed collocation used to indicate that something is of a very high degree, meaning "extremely...", "very...", "exceedingly...", etc. It is often used in both spoken language and written language.

"太……了" is usually composed of "太" and an adjective or adverb, forming an independent sentence or appearing as a subject, object, attributive, or adverbial in a sentence.

"太……了" can be used to describe the degree of various things. Its usage is simple and flexible, depicting a strong feeling, but when using it, attention should be paid to the context and tone, to avoid being too exaggerated or blunt in expression.

（1）这个节目太好看了，我已经看了三遍了。（太好看了，表示非常喜欢这个节目）

（2）今天太热了，我不想出门。（太热了，表示天气非常炎热）

（3）这次考试太难了，我都不知道怎么做。（太难了，表示考试非常困难）

（4）他太优秀了，汉语进步很快。（太优秀了，表示对方非常出色）

三 "已经"的用法 Usage of "已经（yǐjīng）"

"已经"是一个表示过去或现在已经完成的时间副词，常用于表示某个动作或状态已经发生或已经完成。

"已经" is a time adverb that indicates completion in the past or present. It is often used to indicate that an action or state has already occurred or has been completed.

（1）我已经通过海关了。

（2）他已经做完作业了。

（3）我们已经做好准备了。

（4）她已经吃过晚饭了。

四 表示时长的用法 Usage of 时长（shícháng）

汉语中表示询问时长的问法有很多种，常用的有以下几种：

The Chinese language has various ways to inquire about the duration of time, including:

1."几……"：表示时间段的大致范围。例如："你去旅行几天？""我们约好了几点？"。

Using "几……" to indicate a rough range of time, such as"你去旅行几天？"（How many days are you traveling?）and "我们约好了几点？"（What time did we agree on?）.

2."多久"：表示一段时间的长短，常用于询问时间长度。例如："你在这里等了多久？""你打算学习多久？"。

Using "多久" to ask about the length of time, such as "你在这里等了多久？"（How long have you been waiting here?）and "你打算学习多久？"（How long do you plan to study?）.

3."多长时间"：表示一个具体的时间长度。例如："这项工作需要多长时间完成？""火车到达需要多长时间？"。

Using "多长时间" to ask about a specific length of time, such as "这项工作需要多长时间完成？"（How long does it take to complete this task?）and "火车到达需要多长时间？"（How long does the train take to arrive?）.

4."什么时候"：表示时间点或某个时间的具体情况。例如："你什么时候到达机场？""明天你什么时候开始上班？"。

Using "什么时候" to ask about a specific time or event, such as "你什么时候到达机场？"（When will you arrive at the airport?）and "明天你什么时候开始上班？"（When do you start work tomorrow?）.

5.“花多少时间”：表示完成某项任务或活动所需的时间。例如：“你完成这个项目花了多少时间？”“他们花了多少时间准备晚会？”。

Using "花多少时间" to ask about the time spent to complete a certain task or activity, such as "你完成这个项目花了多少时间？" (How much time did you spend completing this project?) and "他们花了多少时间准备晚会？" (How much time did they spend preparing for the party?).

课后练习 Exercises

一 **看拼音写汉字**。Look at the pinyin and write the words.

zhèng jiàn	mào zi	dǎ suàn	zhù	shùn lì
( )	( )	( )	( )	( )

tōng guò	chū kǒu	jiāo tōng	fāng biàn	dì tiě
( )	( )	( )	( )	( )

二 **选词填空**。Choose the correct word to fill in the blanks.

海关人员　　　出发　　　配合　　　多长时间　　　顺利

1. 祝你工作（　　　）。

2. 我们现在（　　　）去上海。

3. 谢谢您的（　　　）。

4. 你还要（　　　）可以到学校？

5. 我正在回答（　　　）的问题。

三 **把下面的词语整理成句子**。Rearrange the following words and phrases to make sentences.

1. 几点　　我们　　出发

2. 太热　　今天　　了

3. 到了　　已经　　他

4. 方便　　地铁　　这里的　　很

5. 在　　这里　　我　　等　　你

四 **回答问题。** Answer the questions.

1. 出入境需要检查护照吗？

_____

2. 持旅游签证可以在中国待多长时间？

_____

3. 接机的人可以在机场什么地方等？

_____

4. 通过海关的时候需要注意什么？

_____

5. 从机场到市区的交通一般有哪些？

_____

五 **听录音，判断对错。** Listen to the recording and judge whether the statements are correct or incorrect.

1. 男生还没通过海关。　　　　　☐

2. 男生是游客。　　　　　　　　☐

3. 女生在三号出口等。　　　　　☐

4. 男生现在在等行李。　　　　　☐

5. 他们坐地铁去学校。　　　　　☐

旅游小贴士 **Travel Tips**

● 一　**购买机票注意事项**[1]

外国旅客在国内乘坐飞机可选择在航空公司官方APP、航空公司小程序等购票平台在线预订飞机票。

1. 购票

（1）通过航空公司官方APP、小程序购票，可采用支付宝、微信、银联银行卡等支付。

（2）在机场窗口购票，可以使用现金、微信、支付宝、银行卡等支付票款，具体以航空公司规定为准。

2. 改签和退票

外国旅客可通过购票平台或机场窗口进行改签或退票。改签或退票可能产生费用，具体以航空公司规定为准。

● 二　**在华工作生活期间注意事项**

1. 关注签证有效期

持签证入境，计划在中国境内工作、生活的，自入境之日起30日内根据条件换成居留许可；若需要延长签证停留期限的，应当在签证注明的停留期限届满

1　本篇内容参考了《外国商务人士在华工作生活指引（2024年版）》及其英文版，详见：https://m.mofcom.gov.cn/article/zwgk/gkbnjg/202401/20240103468871. shtml.

7 日前向停留地县级以上地方人民政府公安机关出入境管理部门申请，按照要求提交申请事由的相关材料。

2. 关注居留许可有效期

居留许可期满后继续停留的，需在有效期满前 30 日之后申请延期。持有效居留许可，若更换新护照或其他居留证件登记事项发生变动的，需在 10 日内到公安机关出入境管理部门申请办理信息变更。

3. 关注工作许可有效期

（1）外国人在中国境内工作应当取得工作许可。来华工作 90 日（含 90 日以下）的，持《外国人工作许可通知》向中国驻外使（领）馆申请 Z 字签证，按照签证标注的时间在华工作。来华工作 90 日以上的，持《外国人工作许可通知》向中国驻外使（领）馆申请 Z 字签证，入境后 30 日内向工作单位所在地外国人来华工作管理部门申领《外国人工作许可证》，按照标注的有效期在华工作。

（2）《外国人工作许可证》有效期届满 30 日前，应当向工作单位所在地外国人来华工作管理部门提出延期申请。

（3）若个人信息（姓名、护照号、职务）等事项发生变更，应自变更事项发生之日起 10 个工作日内，向工作单位所在地外国人来华工作管理部门申请变更。

Purchasing Air Tickets in China: Important Considerations

Foreign travelers in China can choose to book their airline tickets online through the airline's official App or airline mini-programs.

1. Ticket Purchase

(1) Tickets can be purchased through the airline's official app or mini-programs using Alipay, WeChat, or UnionPay bank cards etc..

(2) At the airport ticket counter, tickets can be paid for using cash, WeChat, Alipay, or bank cards..., as per the airline's policies.

2. Changes and Refunds

Foreign travelers can request changes or refunds through the booking platforms or at airport counters. Fees may apply, subject to the airline's policies.

Key Considerations During Work and Stay in China

1. Visa Validity

Those entering China with a visa and planning to work or live within the country must convert to a residence permit within 30 days of entry if eligible.

If an extension of the visa stay is needed, an application should be made to the local public security bureau's exit-entry administration at the county level or above at least 7 days before the visa's expiration, along with the required supporting documents.

2. Residence Permit Validity

If you wish to continue staying after your residence permit expires, you must apply for an extension 30 days before its expiry.

If you have a valid residence permit and get a new passport or if there are changes in your residence registration, you need to apply for a change of information at the local public security bureau's exit-entry administration within 10 days.

3. Work Permit Validity

（1）Foreign nationals working in China must obtain a work permit. Those working for 90 days or less should apply for a Z visa from a Chinese embassy or consulate abroad using the "Notification Letter for Foreigner's Work Permit" and work in China as per the visa's duration.

（2）Those working for more than 90 days should apply for a Z visa and, within 30 days of entry, obtain a "Foreigner's Work Permit" from the foreign nationals' work management department local to their workplace based on the annotated validity period.

（3）If there are changes in personal information (such as name, passport number, or position), these must be reported to the local foreign nationals' work management department within 10 working days of the change.

第二单元

交通

Unit 2
Transportation

在本单元，你将了解中国目前流行的几种交通工具。你将学习打车时如何与司机交流，乘坐地铁和高铁时如何购票等相关内容的表达，这些都能够帮助你更快地了解如何乘坐不同的交通工具，更方便地进行外出活动。

In this unit, you will learn about several modes of transportation currently used in China. You will learn how to communicate with drivers when taking a taxi, how to purchase tickets when taking the subway and high-speed rail, among other related topics. These will help you quickly understand how to use various forms of transportation, making it easier for you to get around.

第四课

Lesson 4 出租车

Taxi

课前热身 Warm up

1. 你到一个陌生的地方旅游，首先会选择哪一种交通工具？

2. 在你们国家打车都是如何付钱的？

课文 Texts

课文一

A：您好，请问去哪里？

B：您好，我要去开元酒店。

A：好的。

B：机场到酒店开车要多久？

A：如果不堵车，可能四十分钟左右。

B：有点儿远啊。

A：虽然有点儿远，但是这家酒店很不错。

B：真的吗？我很期待。

kèwén yī

A：Nín hǎo, qǐngwèn qù nǎlǐ?

B：Nín hǎo, wǒ yào qù Kāiyuán Jiǔdiàn.

A：Hǎo de.

B：Jīchǎng dào jiǔdiàn kāichē yào duōjiǔ?

A：Rúguǒ bù dǔchē, kěnéng sìshí fēnzhōng zuǒyòu.

B：Yǒudiǎnr yuǎn a.

A：Suīrán yǒudiǎnr yuǎn, dànshì zhè jiā jiǔdiàn hěn búcuò.

B：Zhēn de ma? Wǒ hěn qīdài.

课内练习 Exercises

一 分角色朗读课文。Role-play the conversation.

二 根据课文内容，回答问题。Answer questions according to the text.

    1. B 要去哪里？

    2. 机场到酒店开车要多久？

    3. 这家酒店怎么样？

三 听一听，跟读句子。Listen and read the sentences.

    1. 您好，我要去开元酒店。

    2. 机场到酒店开车要多久？

    3. 如果不堵车，可能四十分钟左右。

    4. 虽然有点儿远，但是这家酒店很不错。

    5. 真的吗？我很期待。

生词学习 New words

您好	nín hǎo	hello
请问	qǐngwèn	excuse me
哪里（代）	nǎlǐ	where
要（动）	yào	want
酒店（名）	jiǔdiàn	hotel
机场（名）	jīchǎng	airport
开车（动）	kāi chē	drive
多久	duō jiǔ	how long
啊（叹）	a	a modal particle used at the end of a sentence as a sign of confirmation or defense
如果（连）	rúguǒ	if
不（副）	bù	not, no

堵车（名）	dǔchē	traffic jam
可能（助）	kěnéng	maybe
分（钟）（名）	fēn（zhōng）	minute
左右（副）	zuǒyòu	about
有点儿（副）	yǒudiǎnr	a little, a bit
虽然（连）	suīrán	although
但是（连）	dànshì	but
家（量）	jiā	used for families or business establishments
不错（形）	búcuò	pretty good
真（副）	zhēn	really
很（副）	hěn	very
期待（动）	qīdài	expect

 **课文 Texts**

课文二

A：您好，我们到酒店了。

B：一共多少钱？

A：一共是八十块。您可以扫描二维码付钱。

B：不好意思，能用现金吗？

A：没问题。

B：好的，给您八十块。

A：别忘记带您的行李。

B：好的，谢谢你，再见!

A：再见!

kèwén èr

A：Nín hǎo, wǒmen dào jiǔdiàn le.

B：Yígòng duōshǎo qián？

A：Yígòng shì bāshí kuài. Nín kěyǐ sǎomiáo èrwéimǎ fùqián.

B：Bù hǎoyìsi, néng yòng xiànjīn ma？

A：Méi wèntí.

B：Hǎo de, gěi nín bāshí kuài.

A：Bié wàngjì dài nín de xíngli.

B：Hǎo de, xièxie nǐ, zàijiàn！

A：Zàijiàn！

课内练习 Exercises

一　分角色朗读课文。Role-play the conversation.

二　根据课文内容，回答问题。Answer questions according to the text.

　　1. B需要付多少钱？

　　2. B是现金支付吗？

　　3. 司机提醒B什么？

三　听一听，跟读句子。Listen and read the sentences.

　　1. 一共多少钱？

　　2. 不好意思，能用现金吗？

　　3. 没问题。

　　4. 别忘记带您的行李。

　　5. 好的，谢谢你，再见！

生词学习 New words

我们（代）	wǒmen	we, us
到（动）	dào	arrive
一共（副）	yígòng	in total
多少（代）	duōshǎo	how much, how many
可以（助）	kěyǐ	can
扫描（动）	sǎomiáo	scan
二维码（名）	èrwéimǎ	QR code
付（动）	fù	pay
不好意思	bù hǎoyìsi	sorry
能（助）	néng	can
用（动）	yòng	use
现金（名）	xiànjīn	cash
没问题	méi wèntí	no problem
没（有）（动）	méi（yǒu）	do not have
块（量）	kuài	a unit of money, same as "yuan"
别（副）	bié	don't
忘记（动）	wàngjì	forget
带（动）	dài	bring
再见（动）	zàijiàn	goodbye

语言点链接 Language points

- "可能"的用法 Usage of "可能（kěnéng）"

  "可能"表示也许、或许。可以用在动词或者主语前面。

  The word "可能" means maybe or perhaps, and can be used before a verb or a subject.

  （1）他可能是美国人。

（2）她可能生病了。

（3）这里可能堵车了。

（4）她可能喜欢喝咖啡。

二 "有点儿"的用法 Usage of "有点儿（yǒudiǎnr）"

一般的用法是"有点儿＋形容词/动词"，表达一种对人或者事物不满意、不喜欢的情绪。

The general structure is "有点儿＋adj./v.", which expresses a feeling of dissatisfaction or dislike towards a person or thing.

（1）今天有点儿冷。

（2）我昨天有点儿生气。

（3）这个地方人有点儿多。

（4）老师有点儿累。

三 "虽然……但是……"的用法 Usage of "虽然（suīrán）……但是（dànshì）……"

"虽然……但是……"连接两个分句，是表达转折关系的两个关联词。

The conjunctions "虽然……但是……" connect two clauses, creating an adversative relationship.

（1）蚂蚁虽然很小，但是力气很大。

（2）虽然汉语有点儿难，但是她很喜欢学习汉语。

（3）虽然今天是周末，但是她还要去上班。

（4）虽然今天是晴天，但是感觉很冷。

四 "了"的用法 Usage of "了（le）"

助词"了"表示动作的完成与实现，一般结构为"动词＋了"。

The particle "了" indicates the completion or realization of an action, following the general structure "v.＋了".

（1）他写了汉字。

（2）我们到了。

（3）我们吃了晚饭。

（4）他们买了礼物。

五 "能"的用法 Usage of "能（néng）"

"能"表示具备某种能力，还表示主观上能够，后面常跟动词。"能……吗？"常用于表达疑问，意思是请求、希望获得许可。

"能" indicates the possession of a certain ability and also conveys a subjective capability. It is commonly followed by a verb and is often used in the form "能……吗？" to express a question, implying a request or hope for permission.

（1）我能去超市吗？

（2）弟弟能说汉语。

（3）她能做饭。

（4）我能坐这儿吗？

"能"的否定形式一般为"不能"。当有人用"能……吗？"表达请求时，一般肯定的回答是"可以"，礼貌的否定回答是"不好意思+原因"。

The negative form of "能" is generally "不能". When someone makes a request using "能……吗？", a typical affirmative response is "可以", and a polite negative response is "不好意思" followed by the reason.

（1）上课的时候，他不能睡觉。

（2）A：你能教我说汉语吗？

　　　B：可以啊。

（3）A：你能陪我去商场吗？

　　　B：不好意思，我要学习。

六 钱的表达 Usage of currency notation

日常生活中，人民币的单位有元、角、分。其中，"元"在口语中读作"块"。

In daily life, the units of Renminbi (Chinese currency) are "元、角、分", with "元" often replaced by "块" in spoken Chinese.

询问价格时，一般用"……多少钱？"。

When inquiring about prices, the general sentence pattern "……多少钱" (How much is it?) is typically used.

（1）A：这件衣服多少钱？

　　　B：三百二十块。

（2）A：这些一共多少钱？

　　　B：一共五十块。

课后练习　Exercises

一　**看拼音写汉字**。Look at the pinyin and write the words.

èr wéi mǎ	xiàn jīn	zuǒ yòu	sǎo miáo	yígòng
（　　　）	（　　　）	（　　　）	（　　　）	（　　　）

qī dài	jiǔ diàn	dǔ chē	kě néng	yǒu diǎnr
（　　　）	（　　　）	（　　　）	（　　　）	（　　　）

二　**选词填空**。Choose the correct word to fill in the blanks.

付钱	忘记	期待	机场	不错

1. 不要（　　　）带护照。

2. 这个地方很（　　　）。

3. 请问您怎么（　　　）？

4. 他非常（　　　）这次见面。

5. 北京有三个（　　　）。

三 对话配对。Match the sentences.

1　你觉得这个地方怎么样？　　　　A　当然可以。

2　虽然我不是中国人，　　　　　　B　三块。

3　她去哪里了？　　　　　　　　　C　我觉得人有点儿多。

4　能帮帮我吗？　　　　　　　　　D　她去机场了。

5　这瓶水多少钱？　　　　　　　　E　但是我会说汉语。

四 把下面的词语整理成句子。Rearrange the following words and phrases to make sentences.

1. 今天　　　热　　　有点儿

2. 你　　　吃　　　吗　　　了

3. 中国人　　她　　　可能　　　是

4. 分钟　　　开车　　需要　　　30

5. 他　　　汉字　　写　　　能

五 听录音，判断对错。Listen to the recording and judge whether the statements are correct or incorrect.

1. 老师能说英语。　　□

2. 那本汉语书50块。　□

3. 机场离饭店有点儿远。□

4. 男生没有现金。　　□

5. 他要去酒店。　　　□

第五课
Lesson 5　地　铁
Subway

前热身　**Warm up**

1. 在中国，地铁有几种购票方式？

2. 在中国坐地铁的时候，不可以带什么东西？

文　**Texts**

课文一

A：您好，我想去天一阁参观，请问乘坐几号线？

B：您可以乘坐地铁一号线，在西门口站下车。

A：好的，请问怎么买票？

B：您可以在购票机上买票。

A：不好意思，我第一次来宁波，可以教教我吗？

B：您先选择您要下车的地方，然后选择票数，
　　最后付钱就可以了。

A：好的，非常感谢。

B：不客气。

kèwén yī

A：Nín hǎo, wǒ xiǎng qù Tiānyī Gé cānguān, qǐngwèn chéngzuò jǐ hào xiàn ?

B：Nín kěyǐ chéngzuò dìtiě yī hào xiàn, zài Xīménkǒu zhàn xià chē.

A：Hǎo de, qǐngwèn zěnme mǎi piào ?

B：Nín kěyǐ zài gòu piào jī shàng mǎi piào.

A：Bù hǎoyìsi, wǒ dì-yī cì lái Níngbō, kěyǐ jiāojiao wǒ ma ?

B：Nín xiān xuǎnzé nín yào xiàchē de dìfang, ránhòu xuǎnzé piào shù,
　　zuìhòu fù qián jiù kěyǐ le.

A：Hǎo de, fēicháng gǎnxiè.

B：Bú kèqi.

课内练习 Exercises

一 分角色朗读课文。Role-play the conversation.

二 根据课文内容，回答问题。Answer questions according to the text.

    1. A 要去哪里？

    2. A 需要乘坐几号线？

    3. A 是第一次来宁波吗？

    4. A 可以在哪里买票？

三 听一听，跟读句子。Listen and read the sentences.

    1. 您好，我想去天一阁参观，请问乘坐几号线？

    2. 好的，请问怎么买票？

    3. 不好意思，我第一次来宁波，可以教教我吗？

    4. 您先选择您要下车的地方，然后选择票数，最后付钱就可以了。

    5. 好的，非常感谢。

生词学习 New words

天一阁（名）	Tiānyī Gé	Tianyi Pavilion
参观（动）	cānguān	visit
在（介）	zài	at
西门口（名）	Xīménkǒu	West Gate
下车（动）	xiàchē	get off
怎么（代）	zěnme	how
票（名）	piào	ticket
购票机（名）	gòu piào jī	ticket machine
第一（序数）	dì-yī	first
来（动）	lái	come
教（动）	jiāo	teach
先（副）	xiān	first, in advance

选择（动）	xuǎnzé	choose
地方（名）	dìfang	place
然后（连）	ránhòu	then, after that
最后（副）	zuìhòu	last
非常（副）	fēicháng	very, extremely
不客气	bú kèqi	you are welcome

 Texts

课文二

A：您好，您的包需要安检。

B：好的。

A：您包里面是不是有一瓶水？

B：是的，我刚买的矿泉水。

A：因为有些危险液体不可以带上地铁，
　　所以需要您试喝一下。

B：好的，没问题。

A：感谢您的配合。

kèwén èr

A：Nín hǎo, nín de bāo xūyào ānjiǎn.

B：Hǎo de.

A：Nín bāo lǐmiàn shì búshì yǒu yì píng shuǐ？

B：Shì de, wǒ gāng mǎi de kuàngquánshuǐ.

A：Yīnwèi yǒuxiē wēixiǎn yètǐ bù kěyǐ dàishàng dìtiě,

　　suǒyǐ xūyào nín shì hē yíxià.

B：Hǎo de, méi wèntí.

A：Gǎnxiè nín de pèihé.

课内练习 Exercises

一　分角色朗读课文。Role-play the conversation.

二　根据课文内容，回答问题。Answer questions according to the text.

　　1. A包里面有什么？

　　2. A刚买了什么东西？

　　3. B需要A做什么？

三　听一听，跟读句子。Listen and read the sentences.

　　1. 您包里面是不是有一瓶水？

　　2. 是的，我刚买的矿泉水。

　　3. 因为有些危险液体不可以带上地铁，所以需要您试喝一下。

　　4. 好的，没问题。

　　5. 感谢您的配合。

生词学习 New words

包（名）	bāo	bag
需要（动）	xūyào	need
里面（名）	lǐmiàn	inside
是（动）	shì	be
一瓶水	yì píng shuǐ	a bottle of water
刚（副）	gāng	just
矿泉水（名）	kuàngquánshuǐ	mineral water
因为（连）	yīnwèi	because
危险（形）	wēixiǎn	dangerous
液体（名）	yètǐ	liquid
所以（连）	suǒyǐ	therefore
试（动）	shì	try
喝（动）	hē	drink
一下（量）	yíxià	used after a verb, indicating an act or an attempt

语言点链接 Language points

一　连动句的用法 Usage of 连动句（lián dòng jù）

连动句是指连动短语充当谓语的句子，或者是由连动短语直接构成的句子。短语的位置顺序不能相互颠倒，中间也没有语音停顿。它们可以分别连着主语单用。后一个动作可以表示前一个动作的目的。第一个动词后表示地点的宾语有时可以省略。

模式之一："去＋地方＋做什么"。表示去某个地方做某件事情。

A serial verb construction is a sentence in which a series of verb phrases act as the predicate, or the sentence is directly composed of these verb phrases. The order of the phrases cannot be reversed, and there are no pauses between them. They can each connect directly to the subject. The action described by the later verb can indicate the purpose of the action described by the earlier verb. Sometimes, the object that indicates the location following the first verb can be omitted.

One common pattern is "去＋地方＋做什么". This pattern indicates going to a specific place to do something.

（1）我去商场买衣服。

（2）他去学校上课。

（3）我们去饭店吃饭。

（4）他们去北京旅游。

二　"怎么"的用法 Usage of "怎么（zěnme）"

疑问代词"怎么"用在动词前，表明询问动作的方式。

The interrogative pronoun "怎么" (how) is used before a verb to ask about the manner of an action.

（1）地铁站怎么买票？

（2）这个汉字怎么写？

（3）我们怎么去那里？

（4）乘坐出租车怎么付钱？

三　动词重叠的用法 Usage of 动词重叠（dòngcí chóngdié）

在汉语中，经常用动词重叠的方式来表明一个动作用的时间短、尝试或者反复多次的意思，带有一种轻松的口气，多用于口语中。

模式之一：单音节动词重叠。

In Chinese, verb reduplication is often used to indicate that a verb describes an action that is brief, tried, or repeated multiple times, with a relaxed tone, and is mostly used in spoken Chinese.

One common pattern is: Monosyllabic verb reduplication.

（1）说说

（2）听听

（3）看看

（4）试试

四 "先……然后……" 的用法 Usage of "先（xiān）……然后（ránhòu）……"

"先……然后……"用来表明动作或行为的顺序，表示一个动作在前，另一个动作在后。这种结构常用来描述按步骤进行的程序或按时间顺序列出事件。

The phrase "先……然后……" indicates the sequence of actions or behaviors, with one occurring before the other. It explicitly states that one action is to be completed first, followed by another action.

（1）我先学习汉语，然后学习英语。

（2）她先去中国，然后去俄罗斯。

（3）我先上课，然后去图书馆。

（4）他先洗澡，然后吃早饭。

五 "是不是" 的用法 Usage of "是不是（shì bú shì）"

如果提问的人对某一事实或情况已有比较肯定的猜测或估计，为了进一步得到证实，就可以用"是不是"这种疑问句提问。它一般用在谓语前面，也可以用在句首或句尾。

When someone has a fairly certain guess or estimate about a fact or situation and seeks further confirmation, they can use a question format employing the phrase "是不是". This phrase can be placed before the predicate, at the beginning, or at the end of the sentence.

（1）你是不是喜欢喝茶？

（2）他是不是会说汉语？

（3）我们一起去宁波，是不是？

（4）他们买了几本书，是不是？

六 "因为……所以……"的用法Usage of "因为（yīnwèi）……所以（suǒyǐ）……"

"因为……所以……"是因果关系的关联词，"因为"后边加原因，"所以"表示原因所产生的结果。原因在前，结果在后。使用时可以成对出现，也可以省略其中一个。

The conjunction "因为……所以……" expresses a cause-and-effect relationship in Chinese. "因为" (because) introduces the reason or cause, while "所以" (therefore) indicates the consequence or result that follows from the cause. The reason precedes the result in the sentence. These conjunctions can appear together in a sentence, or one of them can be omitted.

（1）因为他生病了，所以他没来上课。

（2）因为天气不好，所以他们决定待在家。

（3）因为他很忙，所以他不能和我一起吃饭。

（4）因为这里没有地铁，所以他们选择乘坐出租车。

课后练习 Exercises

一 看拼音写汉字。Look at the pinyin and write the words.

méi wèn tí	pèi hé	xū yào	xuǎn zé	ān jiǎn
（　　　）	（　　　）	（　　　）	（　　　）	（　　　）

cān guān	fēi cháng	chéng zuò	xià chē	yì píng shuǐ
（　　　）	（　　　）	（　　　）	（　　　）	（　　　）

二 选词填空。Choose the correct word to fill in the blanks.

因为	需要	参观	乘坐	怎么

1. 您好，欢迎（　　　）本次航班。

2. 买票的时候（　　　）出示你的护照。

3. （　　）今天天气不好，所以我们决定去图书馆。

4. 我想去北京的故宫（　　）。

5. （　　）去上海呢？

三　对话配对。Match the sentences.

1　他是不是美国人？	A　不用谢。
2　因为那里有点儿远，	B　是的。
3　非常感谢！	C　这是我刚买的水。
4　这是什么？	D　我不知道，我们可以问问。
5　我们乘坐几号线？	E　所以她不想去参观了。

四　把下面的词语整理成句子。Rearrange the following words and phrases to make sentences.

1. 听听　你　首　这　歌曲

2. 北京　是不是　想　你　去

3. 请问　票　买　怎么

4. 他　去　看书　想　图书馆

5. 你　学习　可以　汉语　学习

五　听录音，判断对错。Listen to the recording and judge whether the statements are correct or incorrect.

1. 他要乘坐出租车去鼓楼。　☐

2. 他的包里面有一件衣服。　☐

3. 男生是第一次去北京。　☐

4. 男生会用购票机买票。　☐

5. 他想试试中国菜。　☐

第六课
Lesson 6 高 铁
High-speed Rail

 **课前热身 Warm up**

1. 中国的高铁都有哪些服务？

2. 目前世界上最快的高铁是哪一列？

课文 Texts

课文一

A：我想去杭州旅游。

B：好啊，我们怎么去呢？

A：我觉得高铁挺方便的。

B：那我们怎么买票呢？

A：我们可以用手机买或者去售票窗口买票。

（高铁站售票窗口）

A：您好，我要买去杭州的高铁票。

C：好的，是今天出发吗？

A：是的。

C：您要买几点的高铁票？

A：十点左右出发的票有吗？

C：稍等，我帮您看看。

十点四十五分出发的高铁可以吗？

A：可以，我要买两张，这是护照。

C：一共是一百四十二块。

kèwén yī

A：Wǒ xiǎng qù Hángzhōu lǚyóu.

B：Hǎo a, wǒmen zěnme qù ne？

A：Wǒ juéde gāotiě tǐng fāngbiàn de.

B：Nà wǒmen zěnme mǎi piào ne？

A：Wǒmen kěyǐ yòng shǒujī mǎi huòzhě qù shòupiào chuāngkǒu mǎi piào.

（Gāotiě zhàn shòupiào chuāngkǒu）

A：Nín hǎo, wǒ yào mǎi qù Hángzhōu de gāotiě piào.

C：Hǎo de, shì jīntiān chūfā ma？

A：Shì de.

C：Nín yào mǎi jǐ diǎn de gāotiě piào？

A：Shí diǎn zuǒyòu chūfā de piào yǒu ma？

C：Shāoděng, wǒ bāng nín kànkan.

　　Shí diǎn sìshíwǔ fēn chūfā de gāotiě kěyǐ ma？

A：Kěyǐ, wǒ yào mǎi liǎng zhāng, zhè shì hùzhào.

C：Yígòng shì yìbǎi sìshíèr kuài.

课内练习 Exercises

一　**分角色朗读课文**。Role-play the conversation.

二　**根据课文内容，回答问题**。Answer questions according to the text.

　　1. 他们准备去哪里？

　　2. 他们要买几点的票？

　　3. 他们买了几张票？

　　4. 一共需要多少钱？

三　**听一听，跟读句子**。Listen and read the sentences.

　　1. 我想去杭州旅游。

　　2. 我觉得高铁挺方便的。

　　3. 那我们怎么买票呢？

　　4. 好的，是今天出发吗？

　　5. 可以，我要买两张，这是护照。

生词学习　New words

杭州（名）	Hángzhōu	Hangzhou
旅游（动）	lǚyóu	travel
呢（助）	ne	used at the end of a question
觉得（动）	juéde	think
高铁（名）	gāotiě	high-speed rail
挺（副）	tǐng	quite
手机（名）	shǒujī	mobile phone
或者（连）	huòzhě	or
售票窗口（名）	shòupiào chuāngkǒu	ticket window
今天（名）	jīntiān	today
几（代）	jǐ	how many
稍等	shāoděng	wait a moment
看（动）	kàn	look at
点（量）	diǎn	o'clock
两（量）	liǎng	two

课文　Texts

A：我们一个小时就可以到杭州了！

B：中国高铁速度最快可以达到
三百五十千米每小时，
中国高铁的速度比我们的快。

A：是啊，中国的高铁又快又安全。

B：听说还可以点外卖。

A：真的吗？中国高铁的服务越来越好了。

B：下次我们可以试试。

A：好主意！

kèwén èr

A：Wǒmen yí gè xiǎoshí jiù kěyǐ dào Hángzhōu le！

B：Zhōngguó gāotiě sùdù zuì kuài kěyǐ dádào

sānbǎi wǔshí qiānmǐ měi xiǎoshí,

Zhōngguó gāotiě de sùdù bǐ wǒmen de kuài.

A：Shì a, Zhōngguó de gāotiě yòu kuài yòu ānquán.

B：Tīngshuō hái kěyǐ diǎn wàimài.

A：Zhēn de ma？ Zhōngguó gāotiě de fúwù yuè lái yuè hǎo le.

B：Xiàcì wǒmen kěyǐ shìshi.

A：Hǎo zhǔyi！

课内练习 Exercises

一 分角色朗读课文。Role-play the conversation.

二 根据课文内容，回答问题。Answer questions according to the text.

1. 到杭州需要多长时间？

2. 中国高铁怎么样？

3. 中国高铁上可以点外卖吗？

4. 中国高铁服务怎么样？

三 听一听，跟读句子。Listen and read the sentences.

1. 我们一个小时就可以到杭州了！

2. 中国高铁的速度比我们的快。

3. 是啊，中国的高铁又快又安全。

4. 真的吗？中国高铁的服务越来越好了。

5. 好主意！

生词学习 New words

小时（名）	xiǎoshí	hour
就（副）	jiù	used to indicate a conclusion or resolution
中国（名）	Zhōngguó	China
时速（名）	shísù	speed per hour
最（副）	zuì	most, to the greatest extent
快（形）	kuài	fast
速度（名）	sùdù	speed
比（介）	bǐ	than, (superior or inferior) to
安全（形）	ānquán	safe
听说（动）	tīngshuō	hear
还（副）	hái	also, too
点（动）	diǎn	order
外卖（名）	wàimài	take-out
服务（名）	fúwù	service
越（副）	yuè	more, to a greater degree
好主意	hǎo zhǔyi	good idea

语言点链接 Language points

一 "挺……的"的用法 Usage of "挺（tǐng）……的（de）"

通常使用的模式是"sth./sb.＋挺＋adj.＋的"。"挺"，副词，意思是"很，相当"。"的"字一定不能省略。

A commonly used structure is "sth./sb.＋挺＋adj.＋的". "挺", an adverb, means "very" or "quite". The word "的" must not be omitted.

（1）她挺聪明的。

（2）公园挺漂亮的。

（3）这本书挺便宜的。

（4）我挺开心的。

二 "那" 的用法 Usage of "那 (nà) "

连词 "那" ，放在句首，表示依据上文的意思得出的结果或做出的判断。

The conjunction " 那 " , when placed at the beginning of a sentence, indicates a conclusion or judgment derived from the preceding context.

（1）A：我不想去看电影。

　　 B：那我也不去了。

（2）A：我生病了。

　　 B：那你需要休息。

三 "就" 的用法 Usage of "就 (jiù) "

副词 "就" 的用法之一是表示事情比预期发生得更早。通常，"就" 前面会有表示时间的表达。

The adverb "就" has several uses, one of which is to indicate that something happens early or sooner than expected. The word "就" is often preceded by terms specifying time.

（1）我早上六点就起床了。

（2）他下周一就到宁波了。

（3）地铁十分钟就到火车站了。

（4）他晚上八点就睡觉了。

四 比较句的用法 Usage of 比较句 (bǐjiào jù)

两种事物或者人之间进行比较时，需要用到比较句。通常的模式是 "A 比 B+adj."。其中，A 与 B 需要为同一性质的事物。

When comparing two objects or people, comparative sentences are used. The typical pattern is "A 比 B+adj.". Both A and B need to be of the same type or category.

	A	比	B	adj.
1	我的书	比	你的书	多
2	苹果	比	香蕉	贵
3	他	比	我	高
4	老师	比	大卫	大

当你需要表达 A 和 B 在某方面没有差异，或者 A 在某方面不超过 B 时，可以使用比较句的否定形式。这种结构可以通过使用 "没有" 或 "不比" 来构建。

When expressing that there is no difference between A and B in some aspect, or that A does not exceed B in a certain aspect, you can use the negative form of a comparative sentence. This structure can be constructed using 没有 or 不比.

	A	没有 / 不比	B	adj.
1	我	没有	他	聪明
2	手机	没有	电脑	贵
3	我的头发	不比	你的头发	长
4	这里	不比	那里	漂亮

五 "又……又……" 的用法 Usage of "又（yòu）……又（yòu）……"

1. "sth./sb.+ 又 +adj./v.+ 又 +adj./v." 句式通常用来形容事物或者人。句式中的两个形容词需要为同一性质的，如都是夸赞的形容词或者都是批评的形容词。

The Chinese sentence pattern "sth./sb.+ 又 +adj./v.+ 又 +adj./v." is used to describe the attributes or states of things or people. In this structure, the two adjectives or verbs need to share the same quality, such as both being complimentary or both being critical.

2. "sb.+ 又 +v.+ 又 +v." 句式通常用来形容人同时在做两个动作。这种结构强调了两个动作的同时发生，通常突出了个人的多任务处理能力或多样化的活动。

The pattern "sb.+ 又 +v.+ 又 +v." is used to describe a person simultaneously performing two actions. This structure emphasizes the concurrent occurrence of both actions, often highlighting the multitasking ability or engagement in diverse activities of the individual.

（1）坐地铁又方便又便宜。

（2）这个城市又漂亮又干净。

（3）我又跳又唱。

（4）她又哭又笑。

六 "越来越……" 的用法 Usage of "越来越（yuè lái yuè）……"

"越来越……" 这个短语通常用来比较人或事物的数量或程度随着时间的推移而不断发展或变化，是同一事物不同时期或不同条件的比较，强调发展和变化的意义。通常在句尾加上 "了"，表示状态的完成或变化。

The phrase "越来越……" is commonly used to indicate that the quantity or degree of a person or thing is continuously developing or changing over time. It is used to compare the same object or person under different times or conditions, emphasizing the sense of development or change. The phrase often ends with 了 to indicate completion or a change in state.

（1）天气越来越冷了。

（2）学习汉语的人越来越多了。

（3）这里的风景越来越美了。

（4）你越来越漂亮了。

课后练习 Exercises

一 看拼音写汉字。Look at the pinyin and write the words.

hǎo zhǔ yi	lǚ yóu	huò zhě	jué de	shāo děng
（ ）	（ ）	（ ）	（ ）	（ ）

fú wù	xiǎo shí	ān quán	tīng shuō	gāo tiě
（ ）	（ ）	（ ）	（ ）	（ ）

二 选词填空。Choose the correct word to fill in the blanks.

方便	速度	出发	服务	手机

1. 这里乘坐高铁很（   ）。

2. 他想买一部（   ）。

3. 这辆车的（   ）很快。

4. 你觉得这家饭店的（   ）怎么样?

5. 他们什么时候（   ）?

三 对话配对。Match the sentences.

1	我们一起去商场吧!	A	我觉得挺好的。
2	你觉得这个地方怎么样?	B	坐地铁吧，地铁又方便又便宜。
3	我们怎么去那里?	C	那我们几点出发?
4	我今天六点就到了。	D	今天没有昨天冷。
5	今天天气怎么样?	E	这么早!

四 把下面的词语整理成句子。Rearrange the following words and phrases to make sentences.

1. 我　今天　觉得　热　挺　的

2. 10　就　分钟　还有　下课　了

3. 我们的衣服　便宜　比他们的

4. 这里的　便宜　又　新鲜　水果　又

5. 这个　越来越　漂亮　了　地方

五 听录音，判断对错。Listen to the recording and judge whether the statements are correct or incorrect.

1. 那个地方风景挺漂亮的。　☐

2. 男生三岁就会游泳了。　☐

3. 他们又说又笑。　☐

4. 男生十八岁。　☐

5. 男生的汉语越来越好。　☐

旅游小贴士 Travel Tips

中国交通工具"知多少"[1]

一 网约车

1. 你知道中国网约车的平台都有哪些吗？

目前，中国网约车平台有滴滴出行、高德、T3出行、曹操出行等平台。

2. 中国的网约车使用新能源吗？

目前，中国的大部分网约车以电动车为主，这极大减少了碳排放，使它们成为绿色出行的主力

1　本篇参考了中国铁路 12306（12306 China Railway）网站的部分内容，详见：https://kyfw.12306.cn/otn/gonggao/saleTicketMeans.html?linktypeid=means2.

军。新能源汽车的车牌统一为绿色。

3. 网约车的支付方式有哪些？

目前，网约车可以通过微信、支付宝或者现金的方式进行支付。

二 高铁

1. 你知道高铁如何购票吗？高铁票可以退票和改签吗？

旅客可通过 12306 官方网站（含"铁路 12306"手机 APP）、车站的售票窗口、自动售票机购买车票。一张车票可以办理一次改签。车票改签后，旅客取消旅行的，可以按规定退票，但开车后改签的车票不能退票。

2. 你知道中国高铁的座位有几种类型？

目前中国高铁座位分为三种，一是商务座，二是一等座，三是二等座。价格由高到低排列。

3. 你知道中国的主要高铁类型吗？

目前中国高铁主要有两种：一是和谐号，二是复兴号。和谐号最高时速达到 350 公里，平均时速大概是 200 公里。复兴号最高时速可以达到 400 公里及以上，持续保持速度是 350 公里。复兴号全车都是覆盖 Wi-Fi 的，不需要额外收取费用，和谐号列车上不会提供 Wi-Fi。

4. 你知道中国高铁服务有什么吗？

（1）提供接送站/机、实时打车等约车服务。

（2）提供便民托运服务。

（3）提供遗失物品查找服务。

（4）提供重点乘客预约服务。

（5）提供中国铁路旅游服务。

（6）提供餐饮配餐服务。

5. 你知道乘坐高铁需要注意什么吗？

（1）不可以抽烟，电子烟也不可以。

（2）扰乱铁路站车运输秩序且危及铁路安全的行为也不可以做，如扒门等干扰列车正常运行的行为。

How much do you know about Chinese transportation?

China's Ride-Hailing Platforms

1. What ride-hailing platforms are available in China?

Currently, China's ride-hailing platforms include DiDi Travel, Amap, T3 Travel, CaoCao Travel, and others.

2. Do ride-hailing services in China use new energy vehicles?

At present, most ride-hailing vehicles in China primarily use electric vehicles, significantly reducing carbon emissions and establishing them as a main force in green transportation. The license plates for new energy vehicles are uniformly green.

3. What are the payment methods for ride-hailing services?

Currently, ride-hailing services can be paid for using WeChat, Alipay, or cash.

High-Speed Rail in China

1. How to buy tickets for high-speed trains? Can high-speed rail tickets be refunded or changed?

Passengers can purchase tickets through the official 12306 website (including the Railway 12306 mobile APP), at ticket counters in stations, or via automatic ticket machines. Each ticket can be rescheduled once. If the passenger decides to cancel the trip after changing the ticket, they are eligible for a refund, subject to prevailing regulations. However, tickets altered after the departure of the train are non-refundable.

2. What are the different types of seats on chinese high-speed trains?

Currently, Chinese high-speed trains offer three types of seating: business class, first class, and second class, listed in descending order of price.

3. What are the main types of high-speed trains in China?

There are two principal types of high-speed trains in China: the Hexie (harmony) and the Fuxing (revival). Hexie trains can reach a maximum speed of 350 km/h, with an average speed of about 200 km/h. Fuxing trains can attain speeds exceeding 400 km/h and maintain a continuous speed of 350 km/h. The Fuxing trains provide complimentary Wi-Fi coverage throughout the journey, whereas Hexie trains do not offer this service.

4. What services are offered on chinese high-speed trains?

（1）Station/airport pickup and drop-off services, and real-time ride-hailing services.

（2）Convenient baggage handling services.

（3）Lost and found services.

（4）Priority booking services for passengers with special needs.

（5）China Railway travel services.

（6）Onboard catering services.

5. What should you keep in mind when traveling on high-speed trains?

（1）Smoking, including electronic cigarettes, is not allowed.

（2）Actions that disrupt the order of railway station and train operations and jeopardize railway safety, such as blocking train doors or interfering with the normal operation of trains, are also strictly prohibited.

第三单元

酒店

Unit 3
Hotel

在本单元，你会接触到酒店入住、酒店服务和酒店退房的场景。你会学习如何电话预约、办理入住、咨询各项酒店服务、应对突发紧急状况，以及如何完成退房、安排后续行程。学习这些内容可以帮助你完成旅行过程中的住宿安排，提升体验感，融入当地环境，更好地在相应场景下开展交流和沟通。

In this unit, you will encounter scenarios related to hotel check-in, hotel service, and hotel check-out. You'll learn how to make a reservation by phone, handle the check-in, inquire about hotel services, deal with unexpected emergencies, complete the check-out and arrange onward travel plans. Learning these topics will help you manage the accommodation aspect of your travel, improve your experience, immerse yourself into the local environment, and communicate more effectively in relevant situations.

入住

Check in

前热身 **Warm up**

1. 计划出行前，你会如何安排住宿？
2. 预订酒店之前，需要了解哪些信息？

课文 Texts

课文一

A：喂，请问是开元酒店吗？我想预订一个房间。

B：请问就您一位吗？什么时间入住？

A：五月十号入住，十二号退房。

B：稍等一下，我查查是否还有房间。
    还有一间房。

A：房费多少？含早餐吗？

B：一间房五百元，含早餐，
    用餐时间从七点到九点。

A：好，帮我预订一间吧。

B：您确认一下。五月十号到十二号，一个单人间。

A：对的。

kèwén yī

A：Wèi，qǐngwèn shì Kāiyuán Jiǔdiàn ma？ Wǒ xiǎng yùdìng yí gè fáng jiān.

B：Qǐngwèn jiù nín yí wèi ma？ Shénme shíjiān rùzhù？

A：wǔ yuè shí hào rùzhù，shíèr hào tuìfáng.

B：Shāoděng yíxià，wǒ chácha shìfǒu hái yǒu fángjiān.
    Hái yǒu yì jiān fáng.

A：Fángfèi duōshǎo? Hán zǎocān ma？

B：Yì jiān fáng wǔbǎi yuán, hán zǎocān,

　　yòngcān shíjiān cóng qī diǎn dào jiǔ diǎn.

A：Hǎo, bāng wǒ yùdìng yī jiān ba.

B：Nín quèrèn yíxià. Wǔ yuè shí hào dào shíèr hào, yí gè dānrén jiān.

A：Duì de.

课内练习 Exercises

一　**分角色朗读课文**。Role-play the conversation.

二　**根据课文内容，回答问题**。Answer questions according to the text.

　　1. 他要订一间什么房间?

　　2. 他打算住几天?

　　3. 房间多少钱一间?

　　4. 房间包早餐吗?

三　**听一听，跟读句子**。Listen and read the sentences.

　　1. 我想预订一个单人间。

　　2. 早餐时间从七点到九点。

　　3. 稍等一下，我查查是否还有房间。

生词学习 New words

预订（动）	yùdìng	book, reserve
单人间（名）	dānrén jiān	single room
入住（动）	rùzhù	check in
号（名）	hào	number of dates
退房（动）	tuìfáng	check out
查（动）	chá	check
间（量）	jiān	measure word for rooms
房（名）	fáng	room

含（动）	hán	include
早餐（名）	zǎocān	breakfast
从……到……	cóng... dào ...	from... to...
确认（动）	quèrèn	confirm

 课文 Texts

课文二

A：您好，开元酒店。有什么可以帮您？

B：您好，我想登记入住。

A：请问您有预订吗？

B：我预订了一个单人间。

A：好的，麻烦出示一下您的护照。

B：能不能安排一间楼层高一点儿的房间？

A：没问题，请稍等一下。这是房卡。
  您的房间号是一〇〇七，在十楼。

B：好的，谢谢。

A：如果您还需要什么服务，请跟前台联系。
  祝您入住愉快。

kèwén èr

A：Nín hǎo, Kāiyuán Jiǔdiàn. Yǒu shénme kěyǐ bāng nín？

B：Nínhǎo, wǒ xiǎng dēngjì rùzhù.

A：Qǐngwèn nín yǒu yùdìng ma？

B：Wǒ yùdìng le yí gè dānrén jiān.

A：Hǎo de, máfan chūshì yíxià nín de hùzhào.

B：Néng bùnéng ānpái yì jiān lóucéng gāo yì diǎnr de fángjiān?

A：Méi wèntí, qǐng shāoděng yíxià. Zhè shì fángkǎ.
  Nín de fángjiān hào shì yī líng líng qī, zài shí lóu.

B：Hǎo de, xièxie .

A：Rúguǒ nín hái xūyào shénme fúwù, qǐng gēn qiántái liánxì.

　　Zhù nín rùzhù yúkuài.

课内练习 Exercises

一 **分角色朗读课文**。Role-play the conversation.

二 **根据课文内容，回答问题**。Answer questions according to the text.

  1. 他预订了什么房间？

  2. 他对房间有什么要求？

  3. 他的房间在几楼？

三 **听一听，跟读句子**。Listen and read the sentences.

  1. 我想登记入住。

  2. 麻烦出示一下您的护照。

  3. 我预订了一个单人间。

  4. 能不能安排一间楼层高一点儿的房间？

  5. 祝您入住愉快。

生词学习 New words

登记（动）	dēngjì	register
个（量）	gè	measure word
麻烦（动）	máfan	bother
安排（动）	ānpái	arrange
楼层（名）	lóucéng	floor
高（形）	gāo	tall, high
一点儿（副）	yì diǎnr	a little
房间（名）	fángjiān	room
房卡（名）	fángkǎ	room card
号（名）	hào	number

旅游汉语

楼（名）	lóu	floor
如果（连）	rúguǒ	if
需要（动）	xūyào	need
服务（名）	fúwù	service
前台（名）	qiántái	reception
联系（动）	liánxì	contact
愉快（形）	yúkuài	pleased

语言点链接 Language points

一 动词重叠的用法 Usage of 动词重叠（dòngcí chóngdié）

汉语中一些动词可以重叠，动词的重叠形式可以表示时间短、少量、轻微、尝试的意思，语气比较轻松随意，多用于口语。

In Chinese, verbs can be reduplicated. The reduplicative form of a verb indicates a short time, a small quantity, a slight degree or an attempt, conveying a relaxed and casual mood. It is often used in spoken Chinese.

1. 单音节动词的重叠形式：A（一）A

Reduplicative forms of monosyllabic verb: A（一）A

A	AA	A一A
看	看看	看一看
查	查查	查一查
说	说说	说一说

（1）可以让我看看您的护照吗？
（2）麻烦帮我查查我的航班。
（3）小王，你说一说你的想法。

2. 大部分双音节动词的重叠形式：ABAB

Reduplicative forms of most disyllabic verbs: ABAB

AB	AB
休息	休息休息
认识	认识认识

（1）太累了，我们先休息休息再继续吧。

（2）这位是谁？介绍我们认识认识吧。

3. 离合词的重叠方式：AAB

Reduplicative forms of separable words: AAB

离合词指的是词中间可以插入其他成分的词。

Separable verbs get their name from their ability to "separate" into two parts.

AB	ABB
见面	见见面
聊天	聊聊天
帮忙	帮帮忙

（1）周末我喜欢跟朋友见见面、聊聊天。

（2）他一个人忙不过来，你帮帮忙吧。

二 日期的表达Date expressions

汉语的日期表达方式遵循由大到小的原则，先说"月"，然后说"日/号"，最后说"星期"。口语一般常用"号"。

The way to say a date in Chinese observes the principle of "the bigger unit coming before the smaller one". The month is said first, then the date and finally the day of the week. In spoken Chinese, "号" is often used instead of 日 to express the date.

（1）9月1号，星期三。

（2）9月2号，星期四。

（3）8月31号，星期二。

三 "一下"的用法Usage of "一下（yíxià）"

"一下"通常用作动词后缀或副词。它有多种语法用法，包括：

1. 表示动作的短暂性：在动词后面加上"一下"可以表示这个动作的时间很短暂。

2. 表示尝试或建议：表示尝试做某事，或者向别人提出建议。

3. 表示加强语气：有时候"一下"也可以用来加强语气，强调某个动作或状态的存在。

需要注意的是，"一下"通常只能用在动词后面，不能单独使用。同时，"一下"的使用也要根据具体语境和场合来确定。

"一下" is commonly used as a verb suffix or adverb and it has multiple grammatical usages, which include:

1. Indicating the brevity of an action: Adding "一下" after a verb indicates that the action is brief.

2. Indicating an attempt or suggestion: Indicate an attempt to do something or a suggestion to someone.

3. Emphasizing a tone: Sometimes "一下" can be used to emphasize a tone, emphasizing the existence of a certain action or state.

It should be noted that "一下" can usually only be used after a verb and cannot be used alone. Also, the use of "一下" should be determined based on the specific context and situation.

（1）有什么问题你可以问一下老师。

（2）这件衣服你可以试一下。

（3）请确认一下，您订的是大床房。

四 介词"从"的用法 Usage of prepositions 从（cóng）

介词"从"引出一段时间、一段路程、一件事情的经过或者一个序列的起点，后面常跟"到"一起搭配使用。

The preposition "从" introduces the starting point of a period of time, a distance, a process or a sequence, often used together with 到.

（1）从北京到上海要坐几个小时的飞机？

（2）他从下星期一开始上班。

（3）健身房开放时间从上午九点半到晚上十点。

五 "吧"的用法 Usage of "吧（ba）"

"吧"是一个汉语助词，它有多种用法。以下是其中几种常见的用法。

"吧" is a Chinese particle that has multiple usages. Here are some common ones.

1. 表示疑问：在陈述句后面加上"吧"，可以将陈述句变成疑问句。

Indicating a question: Adding "吧" after a statement can turn it into a question.

例：你是我们的导游吧？

2. 表示建议：在请求或劝告的话语后面加上"吧"，可以表示委婉地提出建议。

Indicating a suggestion: Adding "吧" after a request or advice can express a suggestion in a polite way.

例：你应该早点出发吧。

3. 表示不确定或推测：在陈述句后面加上"吧"，可以表示不确定或推测。

Expressing uncertainty or conjecture: Adding "吧" after a statement can express uncertainty or conjecture.

例：他今天晚上没来，可能是忙吧。

4. 表示请求：在一个带有动词的陈述句后面加上"吧"，可以委婉地表达请求。

Making a request: Adding "吧" after a sentence with a verb can express a request in a gentle way.

例：你把这个文件发给我吧。

六 "一点儿"的用法 Usage of "一点儿（yì diǎnr）"

"一点儿"是一个汉语量词，有两种用法。

"一点儿" in Chinese is a quantifier and can be used in two ways.

1. 表示数量少，"一"通常可以省略。

It is commonly used to indicate a small amount or quantity. The 一 can be omitted in most cases.

（1）我们喝点儿水吧。

（2）我有一点儿事，不能跟你一起去了。

2. 表示程度上的微小差别，用于有比较意义的句子中。

It also can be used to indicate a slight difference in degree in sentences with a comparative meaning.

（1）听说你生病了，现在好点儿了吗？

（2）这家酒店比上次那家贵点儿，但是服务也好点儿。

课后练习 Exercises

一 看拼音写汉字。Look at the pinyin and write the words.

jiǔ diàn	yù dìng	rù zhù	què rèn
（　　　）	（　　　）	（　　　）	（　　　）

kè rén	gōng sī	tí qián	yā jīn
（　　　）	（　　　）	（　　　）	（　　　）

二 选词填空。Choose the correct word to fill in the blanks.

| 为 | 房间 | 入住 | 取消 | 查 |

1. 请稍等，我帮您（   ）一下。

2. （   ）里的空调坏了，可以来修一下吗？

3. 请你（   ）我们换一些人民币。

4. 我的行程有变，我需要（   ）预订机票。

5. 我打算 3 号（   ），7 号退房。

三 替换画线部分。Replace the underline parts with the given words or phrases.

1. 我想预订一个<u>单人间</u>。

①标准间　　　　②套房　　　　③大床房

_____

2. 包<u>早餐</u>吗？

①晚餐　　　　②停车费　　　　③客房服务

_____

3. 麻烦出示一下您的<u>护照</u>。

①二维码　　　　②身份证　　　　③邀请函

_____

4. 能不能安排一间<u>楼层高一点儿</u>的房间

①带窗户　　　　②无烟　　　　③离电梯远一点儿

_____

四 把下面的词语整理成句子。Rearrange the following words and phrases to make sentences.

1. 想　　一个　　我　　预订　　双人间

2. 帮　　我　　检查检查　　你　　吧

3. 什么　　回来　　时候　　你

4. 从　　6点　　8点半　　时间　　晚餐　　到

5. 要　　护照　　一下　　看　　我

五　**听录音，判断对错**。Listen to the recording and judge whether the statements are correct or incorrect.

1. 他预订的是单人间。　　　　　☐

2. 客人的名字叫张三。　　　　　☐

3. 他的房间号是 303。　　　　　☐

4. 酒店不提供免费早餐。　　　　☐

5. 餐厅在酒店一楼。　　　　　　☐

酒店服务

Hotel Service

 前热身 Warm up

1. 你知道酒店可以提供哪些服务吗？

2. 你最关注的酒店服务是什么？

课文 Texts

课文一

A：服务员，请问哪里可以用餐？

B：餐厅在六楼。不过，您也可以打电话叫餐，服务员会送到房间。

A：那太好了！你们也有叫早服务吗？

B：有，您可以打一二三六，
告诉前台您需要几点起床。

A：对了，房间里有 Wi-Fi 吗？

B：有的，密码是八个八。

A：顺便问一下，哪儿可以换人民币？

B：酒店出门右拐就有一家银行。

A：好的。谢谢。

kèwén yī

A：Fúwùyuán, qǐngwèn nǎlǐ kěyǐ yòngcān?

B：Cāntīng zài liù lóu. Búguò, nín yě kěyǐ dǎ diànhuà jiào cān, fúwùyuán huì
sòng dào fángjiān.

A：Nà tài hǎo le! Nǐmen yě yǒu jiàozǎo fúwù ma?

B：Yǒu, nín kěyǐ dǎ yāo èr sān liù,
gàosù qiántái nín xūyào jǐ diǎn qǐchuáng.

A：Duì le, fángjiān lǐ yǒu Wi-Fi ma?

B：Yǒu de, mìmǎ shì bā gè bā.

A：Shùnbiàn wèn yíxià, nǎr kěyǐ huàn rénmínbì?

B：Jiǔdiàn chūmén yòu guǎi jiù yǒu yī jiā yínháng.

A：Hǎo de. Xièxie.

课内练习 Exercises

一 分角色朗读课文。Role-play the conversation.

二 根据课文内容，回答问题。Answer questions according to the text.

　1. 餐厅在几楼？

　2. 酒店有叫早服务吗？

　3. 房间有 Wi-Fi 吗？

　4. 哪里可以换钱？

三 听一听，跟读句子。Listen and read the sentences.

　1. 服务员，请问哪里可以用餐？

　2. 餐厅在六楼。

　3. 顺便问一下，哪儿可以换人民币？

生词学习 New words

服务员（名）	fúwùyuán	waiter, waitress
用餐	yòngcān	have meals
餐厅（名）	cāntīng	canteen, restaurant
不过（连）	búguò	however
打（动）	dǎ	call
电话（名）	diànhuà	phone
叫（动）	jiào	order
餐（名）	cān	meal
送（动）	sòng	deliver
叫早（名）	jiàozǎo	wake-up call
告诉（动）	gàosù	tell

起床（动）	qǐchuáng	get up
密码（名）	mìmǎ	password
顺便（副）	shùnbiàn	by the way
换（动）	huàn	change
人民币（名）	rénmínbì	RMB
拐（动）	guǎi	turn

课文 Texts

课文二

A：晚上好，这里是前台，请问有什么可以帮您？

B：我把房卡落在房间里了。

A：可以告诉我您的房间号码吗？

B：一〇〇七号房间。

A：请问您的名字是什么？

B：我叫沙地。

A：好的，马上派工作人员过去帮您开门。

B：谢谢。

A：不客气，有问题随时联系前台。

kèwén èr

A：Wǎnshàng hǎo, zhèlǐ shì qiántái, qǐngwèn yǒu shénme kěyǐ bāng nín?

B：Wǒ bǎ fángkǎ là zài fángjiān lǐ le.

A：Kěyǐ gàosù wǒ nín de fángjiān hàomǎ ma?

B：Yī líng líng qī hào fángjiān.

A：Qǐngwèn nín de míngzì shì shénme?

B：Wǒ jiào Shādì.

A：Hǎo de, mǎshàng pài gōngzuò rényuán guòqù bāng nín kāimén.

B：Xièxie.

A：Bú kèqì, yǒu wèntí suíshí liánxì qiántái.

课内练习 Exercises

一 **分角色朗读课文**。Role-play the conversation.

二 **根据课文内容，回答问题**。Answer questions according to the text.

　　1. 他遇到了什么问题？

　　2. 他住哪个房间？

　　3. 他的问题最后解决了吗？

三 **听一听，跟读句子**。Listen and read the sentences.

　　1. 这里是前台，请问有什么可以帮您？

　　2. 我把房卡落在房间里了。

　　3. 可以告诉我您的房间号码吗？

　　4. 有问题随时联系前台。

生词学习 New words

晚上（名）	wǎnshàng	evening
把（介）	bǎ	used when the object is the receiver of the action of the ensuing verb
落（动）	là	leave
号码（名）	hàomǎ	number
马上（副）	mǎshàng	right now
派（动）	pài	send
工作（动）	gōngzuò	work
人员（名）	rényuán	employee, crew
过去（动）	guòqù	go over
开门（动）	kāimén	open the door
问题（名）	wèntí	problem
随时（副）	suíshí	any time

语言点链接 Language points

"在"的用法 Usage of "在（zài）"

"在"用于指示位置，后面常接表示位置的词语。具体用法有以下两种：

在 is used to indicate location and is often followed by words that denote position. The specific uses are as follows:

1. 作为动词，后边加上表示位置的词语做句子的谓语，用于指示人或者事物的位置。

As a verb, "在" is followed by words indicating location to form the predicate of a sentence, used to indicate the position of somebody or something.

（1）您的房间在六楼。

（2）我的护照在房间里。

（3）鞋子在床下面。

2. 作为介词，后边加上表示位置的词语，用于介绍动作行为发生的位置。

"在" can also act as a preposition, used before words indicating location to introduce the place where an action or behavior takes place.

（1）我在房间里休息。

（2）我爸爸在医院工作。

（3）他在银行换钱。

疑问代词"哪儿/哪里"常用于问句，询问人或事物的位置。

The interrogative pronoun "哪儿/哪里" is often used in questions to ask about the location of somebody or something.

（1）请问餐厅在哪儿?

（2）我的杯子在哪里?

（3）你预订的酒店在哪儿?

结果补语"到"的用法 Usage of result complement "到（dào）"

"到"用在动词后，表示动作的结果。"到"表示动作达到预期目标，有了结果。否定形式是"没（有）+v.+到"。

"到" is used after a verb to indicate the result of an action. It signifies that an action has achieved its expected goal or has reached a certain result. The negative form is "没有 + v.+到".

（1）找了半天，我才找到我的手机。

（2）A：你在北京都吃到了什么特色菜啊？

　　　B：导游带我们去吃了北京烤鸭。

（3）已经买不到那本书了，你能帮我找到吗？

三 "可以"的用法 Usage of "可以（kěyǐ）"

情态动词"可以"有两种用法。

The modal verb "可以" has two uses.

1. 表示能够或可能。可以单独回答问题。否定通常用"不能"，不说"不可以"。

可以 indicates an ability or a possibility. It can be used alone to answer a question. The negative form is usually "不能", not "不可以".

（1）大学生可以在假期实习。

（2）我可以陪你去旅游。

（3）明天我不能来。

2. 表示许可。多用于疑问或者否定。表示肯定用"可以"，能单独回答问题。表示否定用"不可以"或者"不能"。

"可以" indicates a permission. It is often used in questions or negative sentences. "可以" means affirmation. It can be used alone to answer a question. "不可以" or "不能" means negation.

（1）A：我可以用一下卫生间吗？

　　　B：可以。

（2）A：房间里可以抽烟吗？

　　　B：不可以。

（3）未成年人不能喝酒。

四 "有"的用法 Usage of "有（yǒu）"

动词"有"可以用于表示存在的句子中，表示某个处所或者位置存在什么。

The verb "有" can be used in an existential sentence to indicate the existence of something in a particular place or location.

（1）酒店附近有一家银行。

（2）我们的房间有窗户。

（3）桌子上有一本书。

"有"的否定形式是"没有"，且宾语不能带数量词。

The negative form of "有" is "没有", and the object in the sentence cannot include a numeral classifier.

（1）房间里没有热水，可以给我们换一间吗？

（2）酒店里没有健身房。

（3）酒店附近没有银行。

课后练习 Exercises

一 **看拼音写汉字**。Look at the pinyin and write the words.

kě yǐ	shùn biàn	qǐ chuáng	cān tīng	diàn huà
（　　）	（　　）	（　　）	（　　）	（　　）

hào mǎ	mǎ shàng	wèn tí	suí shí	gōng zuò
（　　）	（　　）	（　　）	（　　）	（　　）

二 **选词填空**。Choose the correct word to fill in the blanks.

可以	派	拐	一点儿	换

1. 直走，然后往左（　　　），银行就在你的右边。

2. 我喜欢大（　　　）的房间。

3. （　　　）帮我个忙吗？

4. 这次我们（　　　）你代表我们参加。

5. 可以给我（　　　）个房间吗？

三 **对话配对**。Match the sentences.

1 顺便问一下，哪儿可以换人民币？

2 您需要填写登记表并提供有效的身份证明。

3 你好，我想入住酒店。

4 我预订了一个单人间，麻烦查一下。

5 对了，房间里有 Wi-Fi 吗？

A 好的，这是我的护照。

B 有的，密码八个 8。

C 好的。您的房间号是 303，电梯在右手边。

D 请问您预订了房间吗？

E 酒店出门右拐就有一家银行。

四 把下面的词语整理成句子。Rearrange the following words and phrases to make sentences.

1. 这　　衣服　　太　　件　　大　　了

2. 银行　一个　酒店　有　旁边

3. 可以　帮我　房间　打扫　一下　吗

4. 找　护照　你　了　吗　到

5. 在　一楼　健身房　酒店

五 听录音，判断对错。Listen to the recording and judge whether the statements are correct or incorrect.

1. 客人想叫车。

2. 他已经预订了机票。

3. 他没有行李需要托运。

4. 他需要酒店提供叫早服务。

5. 他准备明天晚上出发。

退 房

Check out

前热身 **Warm up**

1. 你了解退房需要办哪些手续吗？

2. 你知道中国酒店的退房时间一般是几点吗？

课文 **Texts**

课文一

A：你好，一〇〇七号房间退房。

B：好的，请把房卡给我。

A：给，我要付多少钱？

B：服务员在查房，请您稍等一下，
请问房间有消费吗？

A：没有。

B：对不起，让您久等了。
您确认一下，两晚，一共九百八十元，
现金或者扫码都可以。

A：付好了。顺便帮我叫个车吧，我要去机场。

B：没问题，您稍等，马上为您叫车。

kèwén yī

A：Nǐ hǎo, yī líng líng qī hào fángjiān tuìfáng.

B：Hǎo de, qǐng bǎ fángkǎ gěi wǒ.

A：Gěi, wǒ yào fù duōshǎo qián？

B：Fúwùyuán zài cháfáng, qǐng nín shāoděng yíxià,

　　qǐngwèn fángjiān yǒu xiāofèi ma？

A：Méiyǒu.

B：Duìbuqǐ, ràng nín jiǔděng le.

　　Nín quèrèn yíxià, liǎng wǎn, yígòng jiǔbǎi bāshí yuán,

　　xiànjīn huòzhě sǎomǎ dōu kěyǐ.

A：Fù hǎo le. Shùnbiàn bāng wǒ jiào gè chē ba, wǒ yào qù jīchǎng.

B：Méi wèntí, nín shāoděng, mǎshàng wèi nín jiào chē.

课内练习 Exercises

一 **分角色朗读课文**。Role-play the conversation.

二 **根据课文内容，回答问题**。Answer questions according to the text.

1. 他打算做什么？

2. 他一共住了多长时间？

3. 他要付多少钱？

4. 他要去哪儿？

三 **听一听，跟读句子**。Listen and read the sentences.

1. 你好，一○○七号房间退房。

2. 顺便帮我叫个车吧，我要去机场。

3. 您稍等，马上为您叫车。

生词学习 New words

退房	tuìfáng	check out
给（介）	gěi	for, to
多少（代）	duōshǎo	how many, how much
消费（动）	xiāofèi	consumption
久（副）	jiǔ	long time
扫码	sǎomǎ	scan the code
为（介）	wèi	for

课文 Texts

 课文二

A：喂，一〇〇七号房间退房，退房时间几点？

B：十二点，请您提前办理退房手续。

A：好的，我想暂时寄存一下行李，
需要额外收费吗？

B：不用的。客人的行李寄存都是免费的。

A：那太好了。

B：您对我们酒店的服务还满意吗？

A：房间挺不错的，要是床再软一点就好了。

B：谢谢您的建议，我们下次会改进的。

kèwén èr

A：Wèi, yī líng líng qī hào fángjiān tuìfáng, tuìfáng shíjiān jǐ diǎn?

B：Shíèr diǎn, qǐng nín tíqián bànlǐ tuìfáng shǒuxù.

A：Hǎo de, wǒ xiǎng zànshí jìcún yíxià xíngli,
xūyào éwài shōufèi ma?

B：Búyòng de. Kèrén de xíngli jìcún dōu shì miǎnfèi de.

A：Nà tài hǎo le.

B：Nín duì wǒmen jiǔdiàn de fúwù hái mǎnyì ma?

A：Fángjiān tǐng búcuò de, yàoshi chuáng zài ruǎn yìdiǎn jiù hǎo le.

B：Xièxie nín de jiànyì, wǒmen xiàcì huì gǎijìn de.

课内练习 Exercises

一 **分角色朗读课文**。Role-play the conversation.

二 **根据课文内容，回答问题**。Answer questions according to the text.

1. 退房时间几点？

2. 寄存行李收费吗？

3. 他对酒店的服务有什么建议？

三 **听一听，跟读句子**。Listen and read the sentences.

1. 请您提前办理退房手续。

2. 我想暂时寄存一下行李。

3. 房间挺不错的。

4. 要是床再软一点就好了。

生词学习 New words

提前（副）	tíqián	ahead of time
办理（动）	bànlǐ	to transact
手续（名）	shǒuxù	procedure
暂时（副）	zànshí	for the moment
寄存（动）	jìcún	deposit
额外（副）	éwài	extra
收费（动）	shōufèi	charge
客人（名）	kèrén	guest
免费（副）	miǎnfèi	free of charge
满意（动）	mǎnyì	satisfy
要是（连）	yàoshi	if
软（形）	ruǎn	soft
建议（动）	jiànyì	suggest
次（量）	cì	time
改进（动）	gǎijìn	improve

语言点链接 Language points

一 疑问代词"多少"的用法Usage of the interrogative pronoun "多少（duōshǎo）"

疑问代词"多少"用于疑问句，询问数量，一般用于询问十以上的数量，后面的量词可以省略。十以下的数量一般用"几"来询问。常见的结构为"S＋多少＋（量词）＋n."。

The interrogative pronoun "多少" is used in interrogative sentences to inquire about quantity, usually for quantities above ten, and the measure word can be omitted. For quantities below ten, "几" is usually used. The common structure is "S＋多少＋(measure word)+n." .

（1）你们公司一共有多少人？

（2）A：门票多少钱一张？

　　　B：一百块。

（3）你在这里待了几天？

（4）我要付多少钱？

二 "给"的用法 Usage of "给（gěi）"

"给"的用法有以下几种：

The word "给" has the following usages:

1. 用作动词，表示让对方得到某物。

As a verb, it means to give something to someone.

（1）过节的时候，中国人喜欢给红包。

（2）我给了他一块手表，作为他的生日礼物。

2. 用作介词，用来引出接受的对象。

As a preposition, it is used to introduce the recipient of something.

（1）我已经给他发了邮件，他还没回复。

（2）有什么问题给我打电话。

3. 用作介词，用来表达替人或者帮人做事，引出动作的受益对象。

As a preposition, it is used to express doing something for someone else or helping someone, introducing the beneficiary of the action.

（1）公司给每位员工都安排了住宿。

（2）我出去旅游时，他给我看家。

三 "还是"和"或者"的用法 Usage of "还是（háishì）" and "或者（huòzhě）"

"还是"用于选择疑问句，通常用于"A还是B"的结构中，要求人们在两个选项中做出选择。回答时通常是选择A或B中的一个。例如：

"还是" is used in alternative questions, generally in the structure of "A还是B", where a choice between two options is required. The response usually involves choosing one of the two options, A or B.

（1）A：你喝茶还是咖啡？

　　　B：我喝咖啡。

（2）你想去北京还是上海？

（3）你喜欢吃甜的还是咸的？

如果是在选择肯定句中，要用"或者"表示两种情况任选其一。

In affirmative sentences with a choice, "或者" is used to indicate that either of the two options can be selected.

（1）您现金或者扫码支付都行。

（2）去吃西餐或者中餐都行，你自己决定吧。

四　"在"的用法 Usage of "在（zài）"

1. "在"表示动作正在进行。动词前边加上副词"在"，表示动作正在进行。口语中常在句末加语气助词"呢"，构成"在……（呢）"结构。

"在" is used to indicate an action in progress. When adding the adverb "在" before a verb, it means that an action is ongoing. In spoken Chinese, it is common to add the modal particle "呢" at the end of a sentence to form the structure "在……（呢）".

（1）别说话，他在休息呢。

（2）外面在下雨，外面还出去吗？

（3）他一直在忙，没有时间吃饭。

2. "没(在)+v./v. phrase"表示否定，句尾不能用"呢"。

The negative form is "没(在)+ v. /v. phrase", where "呢" cannot be used at the end of the sentence.

（1）他没在打电话。

（2）他们没在工作。

五　结果补语"v.+好" Usage of result complement "v.+好（hǎo）"

动词或形容词用在动词后，表示动作的结果。"v.+好"表示动作行为已经完成，并且达到了标准或要求。否定形式是"没（有）+v.+好"。

When a verb or an adjective is used after a verb, it indicates the result of an action. The structure "v.+好" indicates that an action has been completed and meets the required standard or expectation. The negative form is "没（有）+v.+好".

（1）工作我们已经做好了。

（2）房间已经收拾好了，您马上就可以入住。

（3）饭准备好了，快来吃吧！

六 "对" 的用法 Usage of "对（duì）"

介词"对"表示对待，用来引出动作、感情的对象。

The preposition "对" can be used to indicate how someone treats or feels about someone or something, and it introduces the object of the action or emotion.

（1）服务员对所有客人都很热情。

（2）我对这个房间很满意。

（3）要是您对我们的服务有任何意见，请您尽管提。

七 "要是" 的用法 Usage of "要是（yào shi）"

"要是"表示假设，相当于"如果"，常用在口语中，也可以说"要是……的话"。

"要是" indicates a supposition. It is an equivalent to "如果". It is often used in spoken Chinese. Sometimes we use "要是……的话" instead.

（1）要是房间有暖气就好了。

（2）要是没有时间的话，我就不能去旅游了。

（3）要是明天不下雨，我们就去爬山。

课后练习 Exercises

一 看拼音写汉字。Look at the pinyin and write the words.

duō shǎo	huò zhě	xiāo fèi	jī chǎng	yí gòng
（　　）	（　　）	（　　）	（　　）	（　　）

tí qián	bàn lǐ	shōu fèi	mǎn yì	yào shi
（　　）	（　　）	（　　）	（　　）	（　　）

二 选词填空。Choose the correct word to fill in the blanks.

要是	或者	收费	提前	多少

1. 今天（　　）明天都行，只要你能来。

2. 这里停车（　　）吗？

3. 如果你不能入住，请（　　）取消预约。

4. 这次你们派了（　　）人参加比赛？

5. （　　）明天他不来，那我们就取消会议。

三　**替换画线部分**。Replace the underline parts with the given words or phrases.

1. 请把<u>房卡</u>给我。
①护照　　　　　　②身份证　　　　　　③行李
_____

2. <u>现金</u>或者<u>扫码</u>都可以。
①单人间/双人间　　②咖啡/茶　　　　　③这次/下次
_____

3. 请您提前<u>办理退房</u>手续。
①取消预约　　　　　②打电话　　　　　　③通知
_____

4. 要是<u>床再软一点</u>就好了。
①房间有暖气　　　　②被子舒服一点儿　　③楼层高一点儿
_____

四　**把下面的词语整理成句子**。Rearrange the following words and phrases to make sentences.

1. 人　　来　　这次　　多少　　了

2. 给　　妈妈　　我　　买　　花

3. 安排　　行程　　好　　已经　　了

4. 对　　房间　　他　　满意　　很

5. 看书　　他　　在　　呢

五　**听录音，判断对错**。Listen to the recording and judge whether the statements are correct or incorrect.

1. 他想办理入住。　　□

2. 他住 202 房间。　　□

3. 他还要额外付钱。　□

4. 他对酒店很满意。　□

5. 他要去机场。　　　□

旅游小贴士 Travel Tips

酒店

一 中国酒店"知多少"

中国常见的酒店品牌有：

万达酒店集团：万达酒店集团是中国最大的酒店集团之一，旗下有万达嘉华、万达瑞华、万达文华等品牌，拥有国内外多家酒店和度假村。

香格里拉酒店集团：香格里拉酒店集团是亚洲著名的酒店品牌之一，拥有多个酒店品牌，如香格里拉、凯悦、悦榕庄等，遍布全球多个国家和地区。

洲际酒店集团：洲际酒店集团是全球最大的酒店管理公司之一，旗下拥有多个品牌，如洲际、皇冠假日、智选假日等，覆盖全球近 100 个国家和地区。

华住酒店集团：华住酒店集团是中国最大的酒店集团之一，旗下拥有全季、汉庭、7 天等多个知名酒店品牌，分布全国各地。

锦江国际酒店集团：锦江国际酒店集团是中国知名的酒店集团之一，旗下拥有锦江之星等多个酒店品牌，分布全国各地。

希尔顿酒店集团：希尔顿酒店集团是全球著名的酒店品牌之一，在中国市场也有很高的知名度和良好的声誉。在中国，希尔顿酒店旗下有希尔顿逸林、康莱德、华尔道夫等多个品牌。

二 外国人在中国住宿的注意事项

1. 护照和签证

外国人在中国住宿时，需要携带有效的护照和签证等相关证件，以便入住酒店和注册身份。

2. 语言沟通

外国人在中国住宿时，需要注意与酒店员工的语言沟通，尽量使用英语或其他共同语言，以便更好地交流和沟通。

3. 安全问题

外国人在中国住宿时，需要注意自身安全问题，保管好自己的贵重物品，尽量避免在陌生环境下独自外出，以确保自身安全。

4. 用电插头

中国的电源标准为 220V/50Hz，插头类型为三脚扁型插头，外国人需要注意带好相应的插头转换器，以便使用自己的电器设备。

5. 文化礼仪

外国人在中国住宿时，需要注意中国的文化礼仪，尊重当地的习俗和传统，避免在公共场合引起不必要的误解或冲突。

6. 知晓酒店政策

外国人在中国住宿时，需要了解酒店的政策和规定，如退房时间、酒店设施使用规定、安全注意事项等，以免不必要的麻烦和误解。

三　中国酒店一般的入住和退房政策

中国酒店一般的入住和退房政策如下：

1. 入住政策

入住时间：大部分酒店的入住时间为下午 2 点或 3 点，但也有少数酒店的入住时间为中午 12 点或下午 1 点。

入住手续：入住时需提供有效证件，如护照或身份证，并在前台填写入住登记表，支付住宿费用和押金等相关费用。

酒店预订：提前预订酒店可以保证房间的可用性，并可能获得更优惠的房价和折扣。

2. 退房政策

退房时间：大部分酒店的退房时间为中午 12 点，但也有少数酒店的退房时间为下午 1 点或 2 点。

延迟退房：如果需要延迟退房，一般需要向前台咨询并支付额外的费用，具体政策因酒店而异。

退房手续：退房时需要将房间内的物品归还到原位，并办理退房手续，包括结算房费、押金等相关费用。

行李寄存：有些酒店提供行李寄存服务，方便客人在退房后继续游览。

需要注意的是，不同酒店可能存在差异，因此在预订酒店前建议查询酒店的具体政策和规定，并在入住和退房时遵守相关规定，以避免不必要的麻烦。

四 中国酒店一般提供哪些服务

与旅游相关的酒店服务包括以下几个方面：

1. 旅游咨询服务

酒店提供旅游咨询服务，包括当地旅游景点的介绍、交通路线的建议、旅游注意事项等，帮助客人更好地了解当地的文化和风景。

2. 景点门票预订服务

酒店提供景点门票预订服务，让客人不用排队购票，节省时间和精力，同时享受更好的优惠。

3. 包车服务

酒店提供包车服务，帮助客人更方便地游览周边景点，提供舒适、安全和个性化的服务。

4. 租车服务

酒店提供租车服务，帮助客人更加方便地游览周边景点，提供各种品牌、型号和价格的汽车选择。

5. 特色旅游体验

酒店提供特色旅游体验，包括参观当地的特色景点、学习当地的手工艺和文化、品尝当地的美食等，让客人深度了解当地的文化和特色。

6. 住宿套餐服务

酒店提供住宿套餐服务，包括住宿和旅游服务的组合，如住宿加早餐、住宿加景点门票、住宿加餐饮等，让客人更加方便地享受旅游服务。

Hotel

How much do you know about Chinese hotels?

Common hotel brands in China

Wanda Hotels & Resorts: Wanda Hotels & Resorts is one of the largest hotel groups in China, with brands such as Wanda Realm, Wanda Reign, and WandaVista, operating numerous hotels and resorts both domestically and internationally.

Shangri-La Hotels & Resorts: Shangri-La Hotels & Resorts is one of the famous hotel brands in Asia, with multiple hotel brands such as Shangri-La, Hyatt, Banyan Tree, etc., spread across various countries and regions around the world.

Intercontinental Hotels Group: Intercontinental Hotels Group is one of the largest hotel management companies in the world, with multiple brands such as Intercontinental, Crowne Plaza, and Holiday Inn Express, covering nearly 100 countries and regions worldwide.

Huazhu Hotel Group: Huazhu Hotel Group is one of the largest hotel groups in China, with well-known hotel brands such as Ji Hotel, Hanting, and 7 Days Inn, distributed throughout the country.

Jinjiang International Hotel Group: Jinjiang International Hotel Group is one of the well-known hotel groups in China, with multiple hotel brands including Jinjiang Inn, distributed throughout the country.

Hilton Hotels Hotels & Resorts: Hilton Hotels & Resorts is one of the world's famous hotel brands with a strong presence and excellent reputation in the Chinese market. In China, Hilton Hotels has brands including Hilton Garden Inn, Conrad, and Waldorf Astoria.

Important considerations for foreigners staying in China

1. Passport and visa

Foreigners staying in China need to carry valid passports, visas, and other relevant documents for hotel check-in and identity registration.

2. Language communication

When foreigners stay in China, they need to pay attention to language communication with hotel employees and try to use English or other common languages for better communication and interaction.

3. Safety issues

Foreigners should pay attention to their own safety issues, take good care of their valuables, and avoid going out alone in unfamiliar environments to ensure their own safety.

4. Power plugs

The power standard in China is 220V/50Hz, and the plug type is a three-prong flat plug. Foreigners should bring appropriate plug adapters in order to use their own electrical devices.

5. Cultural etiquette

Foreigners should be mindful of Chinese cultural etiquette, respect local customs and traditions, and avoid unnecessary misunderstandings or conflicts in public places.

6. Hotel policies

Foreigners should familiarize themselves with the hotel's policies and regulations, such as check-out times, hotel facility usage regulations, safety precautions, etc., to avoid unnecessary trouble and misunderstandings.

General check-in and check-out policies for Chinese hotels

The general check-in and check-out policies for Chinese hotels are as follows:

1. Check in policy

Check-in time: Most hotels have a check in time of 2pm or 3pm, but there are also a few hotels may allow check in at 12pm or 1pm.

Check in procedures: At check in, you need to present valid documents, such as a passport or ID card, and fill out the check in registration form at the front desk, and pay for the accommodation and any deposit fees.

Hotel reservation: Booking a hotel in advance can ensure room availability and may result in better room rates and discounts.

2. Check out policy

Check out time: Most hotels have a check out time of 12 noon, but there are also a few hotels that have a check out time of 1pm or 2 pm.

Delayed check out: If there is a need for delayed check out, it is generally necessary to consult the front desk and pay additional fees. The specific policy varies depending on the hotel.

Check out procedures: When checking out, it is necessary to return the items in the room to their original places and complete the check out procedures, including settling the room charges and any diposits.

Luggage storage: Some hotels offer luggage storage services to facilitate guests' continued travel after checking out.

Note that different hotels may have varying policies, so it's advisable to check the specific policies and regulations of the hotel before booking and to follow the relevant rules during check in and check out to avoid unnecessary issues.

Common hotel services in China

Hotels often provide tourism-related services include the following aspects:

1. Tourism consulting services

Hotels provide tourism consulting services, including introductions to local tourist attractions, suggestions for transportation routes, travel tips, etc., to help guests better understand the local culture and scenery.

2. Ticket booking service

Hotels provide scenic spot ticket booking services, allowing guests to avoid queues and save time and effort, often with additional discounts.

3. Charter service

Hotels provide charter services to help guests more conveniently visit surrounding attractions, providing comfortable, safe, and personalized services.

4. Car rental services

Hotels provide car rental services to facilitate the exploration of surrounding areas, with options for various brands, models, and price ranges.

5. Featured tourism experience

Hotels provide a unique tourism experience, including visiting local attractions, learning local handicrafts and culture, tasting local cuisine, etc., allowing guests to have a deep understanding of the local culture and characteristics.

6. Accommodation package services

Hotels provide accommodation packages that combine lodging with tourism services, such as accommodation with breakfast, accommodation with attraction tickets, or accommodation with dining, etc., making it more convenient for guests to enjoy tourism services.

活动

Unit 4
Activities

在本单元，你将学习到一些在银行、餐厅和购物场所常用到的语言表达，这些都能够帮助你更快地适应在中国的日常生活。

In this unit, you will learn some language expressions commonly used in banks, restaurants, and shopping places, which can help you adapt more quickly to daily life in China.

第十课

Lesson 10 银 行

Bank

前热身 Warm up

1. 你在什么情况下会去银行？

2. 你有哪家银行的卡，为什么选择了这家银行？

文 Texts

课文一

A：您好，请问您需要办理什么业务？

B：你好，我需要取一千美元现金。

A：好的，请问您预约过了吗？

B：是的，我上周预约的。

A：好的，请您输入密码。

B：让我想想。

A：您好，密码不对，请您再输入一遍。

B：这个呢？

A：这个正确。请您稍等。

B：好的，谢谢。

kèwén yī

A：Nín hǎo, qǐngwèn nín xūyào bànlǐ shénme yèwù?

B：Nǐ hǎo, wǒ xūyào qǔ yìqiān měiyuán xiànjīn.

A：Hǎo de, qǐngwèn nín yùyuē guò le ma?

B：Shì de, wǒ shàng zhōu yùyuē de.

A：Hǎo de, qǐng nín shūrù mìmǎ.

B：Ràng wǒ xiǎngxiang.

A：Nín hǎo, mìmǎ búduì, qǐng nín zài shūrù yíbiàn.

B：Zhège ne？

A：Zhège zhèngquè. Qǐng nín shāoděng.

B：Hǎo de, xièxie.

课内练习 Exercises

一 分角色朗读课文。Role-play the conversation.

二 根据课文内容，回答问题。Answer questions according to the text.

    1. 他们在哪儿？

    2. 你觉得 B 为什么要取现金？

    3. 密码输入了几遍？

三 听一听，跟读句子。Listen and read the sentences.

    1. 请问您需要办理什么业务？

    2. 请您输入密码。

    3. 请您再输入一遍。

    4. 请您稍等。

    5. 让我想想。

生词学习 New words

银行（名）	yínháng	bank
业务（名）	yèwù	business
取（动）	qǔ	withdraw
美元（名）	měi yuán	dollar
输入（动）	shūrù	input
再（副）	zài	again
遍（量）	biàn	measure word
正确（形）	zhèngquè	correct

课文 Texts

课文二

A：您好，请问您需要办理什么业务？

B：你好，我想拉一份流水。

A：好的，您可以在这个机器上直接操作。

B：你可以帮我一下吗？

A：当然可以，这里可以选择时间范围。

B：我需要近三个月的流水。

A：好的，这里按"确定"键就可以了。

B：谢谢你，现在办事比以前方便多了。

kèwén èr

A：Nín hǎo, qǐngwèn nín xūyào bànlǐ shénme yèwù？

B：Nǐ hǎo, wǒ xiǎng lā yí fèn liúshuǐ.

A：Hǎo de, nín kěyǐ zài zhège jīqì shàng zhíjiē cāozuò.

B：Nǐ kěyǐ bāng wǒ yíxià ma？

A：Dāngrán kěyǐ, zhèlǐ kěyǐ xuǎnzé shíjiān fànwéi.

B：Wǒ xūyào jìn sān gè yuè de liúshuǐ.

A：Hǎo de, zhèlǐ àn "quèdìng" jiàn jiù kěyǐ le.

B：Xièxie nǐ, xiànzài bànshì bǐ yǐqián fāngbiàn duō le.

课内练习 Exercises

一 分角色朗读课文。Role-play the conversation.

二 根据课文内容，回答问题。Answer questions according to the text.

1. B需要办理什么业务？

2. 他们是在哪里操作的？柜台还是机器上？

3. B选择的时间范围是什么？

三 听一听，跟读句子。Listen and read the sentences.

1. 您可以在这个机器上直接操作。

2. 你可以帮我一下吗？

3. 当然可以。

4. 这里按"确定"键就可以了。

5. 现在办事越来越方便了。

生词学习　New words

拉（动）	lā	print
份（量）	fèn	measure word
流水（名）	liúshuǐ	deposit and withdrawal transaction records
机器（名）	jīqì	machine
直接（副）	zhíjiē	directly
操作（动）	cāozuò	operate
当然（副）	dāngrán	sure
时间（名）	shíjiān	time
范围（名）	fànwéi	range
近（形）	jìn	now with the time not long ago
按（动）	àn	press with hands or fingers
确定（动）	quèdìng	confirm
键（名）	jiàn	button
办事（动）	bànshì	deal with affairs
以前（名）	yǐqián	past
多（副）	duō	many, much

语言点链接　Language points

一　"让"的用法Usage of "让（ràng）"

　　"让"是动词，表示指使、致使、容许或听任。

　　"让" is a verb, which means to instruct, cause, permit, or allow.

（1）导游让游客在这里等他。

（2）这件事让他难过了很久。

（3）让我仔细想想。

（4）不能再让事情闹大了。

二 **"再"的用法** Usage of "再（zài）"

"再"是一个副词，表示重复或第二次，一般放在动词前表示状态。

"再" is an adverb that indicates repetition or a second occurence, usually placed before a verb to describe the action.

（1）明天我们再继续游宁波。

（2）再来两个菜，老板。

（3）小时候他是个胖子，昨天再见他的时候，他已经瘦了。

（4）别急着决定，我们再商量商量。

三 **"遍"的用法** Usage of "遍（biàn）"

"遍"是一个量词，通常用于表示动作从开始到结束的整个过程，表示次数，可重叠使用。

"遍" is a measure word, which is usually used to indicate the whole process of the action from the beginning to the end. It denotes the number of times something is done and can be used in a repetitive sense.

（1）这书太好看了，我看了两遍。

（2）明天就要演出了，我们再练习两遍吧。

（3）你读一遍肯定没用，读十遍也不一定有用。

（4）他一遍遍叫着妈妈，眼泪止不住地流下来。

四 **"呢"的用法** Usage of "呢（ne）"

"呢"是汉语中常用的语气词,用在疑问句的末尾，表示疑问的语气。在一定的上下文语境里，"呢"前边可以只有一个名词性成分，省去其他成分，包括疑助词。

"呢" is also a commonly used modal particle in Chinese. It is used at the end of the interrogative sentence to indicate a questioning tone. In a certain context, "呢" can be preceded by only one nominal element, omitting other components, including question particles.

（1）我的苹果呢? 刚刚还在桌子上。

（2）这件呢? 那件太花了。

（3）你们俩一起去，我呢?

（4）他们买了礼物。

五 "近"的用法 Usage of "近（jìn）"

"近"是一个形容词，主要用来表示距离很短、在现在之前不长的时间、比较亲密的程度、差别小等意思，多被用来组成与远相对的句子或词组。

"近" is an adjective mainly used to mean a short distance, a short period of time before the present, a degree of intimacy, or a small difference, etc. It is mostly used to form sentences or phrases in contrast with "远"（far）.

（1）这地方很近，我们走过去就可以了。

（2）近几年，宁波发展得很快。

（3）他们最近走得很近啊。

（4）直播间现在有近万人在收看啊。

六 "比"字句的用法 Usage of "比（bǐ）sentence"

"比"字句的形式为"A 比 B+adj.+adv./n."，表示比较的程度差异。

The form of "比 sentence" is "A 比 B+adj.+adv./n.", which indicates a difference in the degree of comparison.

（1）我比他高多了。

（2）他比我胖 6 斤。

（3）这个地方比我住的地方大两倍。

（4）奶奶看起来比去年衰老了许多。

课后练习 Exercises

一 看拼音写汉字。Look at the pinyin and write the words.

xiàn jīn	mì mǎ	yè wù	shū rù	bàn lǐ
（　　）	（　　）	（　　）	（　　）	（　　）

què dìng	cāo zuò	liú shuǐ	fàn wéi	xuǎn zé
（　　）	（　　）	（　　）	（　　）	（　　）

二 选词填空。Choose the correct word to fill in the blanks.

让	近	再	遍	呢

1. 我护照（　　）？刚刚还在包里的。

2. 你（　　）尝尝，现在味道怎么样？

3. 这个商场（　　　）吗?

4. 导游（　　　）我们在这里等她。

5. 我已经说三（　　　）了!

三 对话配对。Match the sentences.

1　您需要办理什么业务?	A　当然可以。
2　请您输入密码。	B　真方便!
3　请问您预约过了吗?	C　让我想想。
4　您可以在机器上操作。	D　我需要一份流水。
5　你可以帮我一下吗?	E　没有。

四 把下面的词语整理成句子。Rearrange the following words and phrases to make sentences.

1. 取　　了　　预约　　我　　今天　　现金

2. 上　　操作　　方便　　机器　　太　　在　　了

3. 看看　　我　　流水　　想　　的　　银行　　这张卡

五 听录音，判断对错。Listen to the recording and judge whether the statements are correct or incorrect.

1. 这位女士在银行拉了半年的流水。　□

2. 这位女士准备出国留学。　□

3. 这位女士忘记了密码。　□

第十一课
Lesson 11 餐 厅
Restaurant

课前热身 Warm up

1. 旅行的时候，你会选择什么样的餐厅吃饭？

2. 查看"饥不择食"这个词语的意思，你曾经有过这样的经历吗？

课文 Texts

课文一

A：欢迎光临！这是我们的菜单。

B：好的，有什么推荐菜吗？

A：我们这儿的油焖笋很受欢迎。

B：好的，那我们尝尝看吧。

A：听您口音，是北方人吧？

B：是的，没吃过这个菜。

A：您可以试试看。

B：好的，就点这个吧。

kèwén yī

A：Huānyíng guānglín! Zhè shì wǒmen de càidān.

B：Hǎo de, yǒu shénme tuījiàn cài ma?

A：Wǒmen zhèr de yóumèn sǔn hěn shòu huānyíng.

B：Hǎo de, nà wǒmen chángchang kàn ba.

A：Tīng nín kǒuyīn, shì běifāng rén ba?

B：Shì de, méi chī guò zhège cài.

A：Nín kěyǐ shìshi kàn.

B：Hǎo de, jiù diǎn zhège ba.

103

课 内练习 Exercises

一 分角色朗读课文。Role-play the conversation.

二 根据课文内容，回答问题。Answer questions according to the text.

    1. 他们在哪儿?

    2. 他们点了什么菜?

    3. 他们是南方人吗?

三 听一听，跟读句子。Listen and read the sentences.

    1. 欢迎光临!

    2. 有什么推荐菜吗?

    3. 听您口音，是北方人吧?

    4. 那我们尝尝看吧。

    5. 您可以试试看。

生 词学习 New words

光临（动）	guānglín	visit
菜单（名）	càidān	menu
推荐（动）	tuījiàn	recommend
菜（名）	cài	dish
油焖笋（名）	yóumèn sǔn	sauteed bamboo shoots
受（动）	shòu	receive
尝（动）	cháng	taste
吧（助）	ba	modal particle at the end of a sentence
听（动）	tīng	listen
口音（名）	kǒuyīn	tone
北方（名）	běifāng	north
吃（动）	chī	eat

 **课文 Texts**

课文二

A：啊，我快饿死了。我们赶紧点菜吧。

B：好的，你吃辣吗？

A：微辣可以。

B：麻婆豆腐怎么样？

A：对我来说有点儿辣。

B：那青椒牛柳吧。

A：太好了。我很喜欢吃牛肉。

B：哈哈，我也是。再来一个番茄炒蛋。

kèwén èr

A：À, wǒ kuài èsǐ le. Wǒmen gǎnjǐn diǎn cài ba.

B：Hǎo de, nǐ chī là ma?

A：Wēilà kěyǐ.

B：Mápódòufu zěnmeyàng?

A：Duì wǒ lái shuō yǒudiǎnr là.

B：Nà Qīngjiāoniúliǔ ba.

A：Tài hǎo le. Wǒ hěn xǐhuan chī niúròu.

B：Hā ha, wǒ yě shì. Zài lái yí gè Fānqiéchǎodàn.

课内练习 Exercises

一　**分角色朗读课文**。Role-play the conversation.

二　**根据课文内容，回答问题**。Answer questions according to the text.

　　1. 他们点了什么菜？

　　2. 他们可以吃辣吗？

　　3. 麻婆豆腐是辣的吗？

三　**听一听，跟读句子**。Listen and read the sentences.

　　1. 我快饿死了。

2. 我们赶紧点菜吧。

3. 麻婆豆腐怎么样？

4. 对我来说有点儿辣。

5. 再来一个番茄炒蛋。

生词学习 New words

快（副）	kuài	soon
饿（形）	è	hungry
死（副）	sǐ	extremely
赶紧（副）	gǎnjǐn	quickly
辣（形）	là	spicy
微（副）	wēi	a little
麻婆豆腐（名）	Mápódòufu	Mapo Tofu
青椒牛柳（名）	Qīngjiāoniúliǔ	Stir-fried Beef with Green Peppers
太（副）	tài	too
喜欢（动）	xǐhuan	like
牛肉（名）	niúròu	beef
哈（助）	hā	the sound of laughter
番茄炒蛋（名）	Fānqiéchǎodàn	Tomato Scrambled Eggs

语言点链接 Language points

一 "动词+什么+名词+语气词" 句式的用法Usage of "v.+什么（shénme）+ n.+int." sentence

"v.+什么+n.+int." 这个汉语疑问句语法结构中，通常省略了主语。在汉语中，特别是在口语和日常交流中，主语经常被省略，尤其是在疑问句和陈述句中。这是因为汉语是一种注重语境和意合的语言，很多时候可以通过上下文或语境来推断出主语。

In the grammatical structure of this Chinese interrogative sentence "v.+什么+ n.+int.", the subject is usually omitted. In Chinese, especially in spoken language and daily communication, the subject is often omitted, especially in interrogative sentences and declarative sentences. This is because Chinese is a language that relies heavily on context and implicit meaning, and the subject can often be inferred from the context or situational cues.

（1）A：我没接到你电话，刚刚在上课。

　　　B：你上什么课呢？今天周六！

（2）A：宁波有什么好吃的吗？

　　　B：太多了！你来了就知道了。

二　"看"的用法 Usage of "看（kàn）"

"看"是一个助词，放在动词后，表示试一试。

"看" is a particle, when used after a verb, it means "to have a try".

（1）尝尝看，这是我妈的拿手菜。

（2）你们俩到底谁跑得快，比比看！

（3）这裙子不错，你试试看。

（4）虽然最近公司请假很难，但是你也可以请请看。

三　"吧"的用法 Usage of "吧（ba）"

"吧"是一个句末语气助词，表示两种意思。第一种表示提议、商量等语气；第二种表示不敢完全肯定的怀疑语气。

"吧" is a modal particle at the end of a sentence, which expresses two meanings. The first meaning is to indicate a tone of proposal, discussion, etc., and the second is to express a tone of doubt or uncertainty.

（1）下次一起去北京玩儿几天吧。

（2）明天再说吧，今天太晚了。

（3）昨天给我打电话的人是你吧？

（4）他去中国了吧？好久没见到他了。

四　"快……了"的用法 Usage of "快（kuài）……了（le）"

"快……了"这种用法通常表示时间或某个事件即将到来或发生，是一个简略的表达方式。可以表示某个活动即将开始，或者某个物品即将送到。它可以根据语境来表示不同的含义。

The construction "快……了" usually indicates that a certain time or event is coming up or imminent, and it is a concise expression. It can indicate that an activity is about to begin or an item is about to be delivered. The specific meaning can vary according to the context.

（1）赶紧吃完，电影快开始了。

（2）别着急，饭快做好了。

（3）放心吧，我快到家了。

（4）我快四十岁了。

五 "怎么样" 的用法 Usage of "怎么样（zěnmeyàng）"

"怎么样" 这个词组在不同的语境中可以有不同的含义和用法，需要根据上下文具体理解。如询问意见或看法、询问情况或状况、询问程度、询问方式等。

The phrase "怎么样" can have different meanings and usages depending on the context, which need to be understood based on the specific situation, such as asking for opinions or viewpoints, inquiring about the situation, asking about the degree, asking about how something is done or the manner of doing it, and so on.

（1）你觉得这个主意怎么样？

（2）你今天怎么样？

（3）他的表演怎么样？

（4）怎么样，用这个方案可行吗？

六 "对……来说" 的用法 Usage of "对（duì）……来说（lái shuō）"

"对……来说" 是一个表示对比、区别或相对关系的短语，通常用于表达某件事情、某种情况或某个观点对于特定人或群体的影响或意义。

"对……来说" is a phrase that expresses contrast, difference, or relative relationship, and is usually used to indicate the influence or significance of a certain thing, situation, or viewpoint for a particular person or group.

（1）对我来说，健康比财富更重要。

（2）对他来说，运动是一种享受。

（3）这个问题对我们公司来说非常重要。

（4）这份任务对他来说很难。

七 "我也是" 的用法 Usage of "我也是（wǒ yě shì）"

"我也是" 通常用于回答别人的问题或陈述，表示自己和对方的情况相同，或者表示自己也有同样的感受、体验、想法等等。这个短语常用于口语交流中，可以用于不同场合和语境。

"我也是" is often used to answer other people's questions or statements, indicating that they are in the same situation, or that they have the same feelings, experiences, thoughts, and so on. This phrase is often used in oral communication and can be used in various situations and contexts.

（1）A：我最近常常加班，真的很累。

　　　B：我也是，我也一样感到很累。

（2）A：你喜欢吃辣的吗？

　　　B：我也是，我也很喜欢吃辣的。

（3）A：这个电影非常好看，我觉得很有意思。

　　　B：我也是，我也非常喜欢这部电影。

课后练习 Exercises

一　看拼音写汉字。Look at the pinyin and write the words.

huān yíng guāng lín　　　　　kǒu qì　　　　bēi fāng　　　diǎn cài

（　　　　　　　　）　（　　　　）　（　　　　）　（　　　　）

gǎn jǐn　　　xǐ huan　　　cài dān　　　tuī jiàn　　　cān tīng

（　　　）　（　　　）　（　　　）　（　　　）　（　　　）

二　选词填空。Choose the correct word to fill in the blanks.

欢迎	看	口气	点	喜欢

1. 听你的（　　　），刚来中国吗？

2. 尝尝（　　　），味道怎么样？

3. 这个餐厅很受（　　　）。

4. 游客很（　　　）在这里拍照。

5. 谁（　　　）的菜？太辣了！

三　对话配对。Match the sentences.

1　没吃过这个菜。　　　　　A　有什么推荐菜吗？

2　这是我们的菜单。　　　　B　微辣可以。

3　你吃辣吗？　　　　　　　C　您可以试试看。

4　这个地方怎么样？　　　　D　我也是。

5　我很喜欢这个餐厅。　　　E　太远了！

四 填写正确的菜肴名。Fill in the correct dish names.

A

B

C

D

A：_____

B：_____

C：_____

D：_____

五 听录音，判断对错。Listen to the recording and judge whether the statements are correct or incorrect.

1.上周二他们在家里吃晚饭。　　　□

2.他们很喜欢这家饭馆的菜。　　　□

3.饭馆很近，走路一分钟就到了。　□

前热身 Warm up

1. 旅行的时候，你会买什么东西回家？

2. 你去过哪些地方旅行，买过什么有意思的东西吗？

课文 Texts

课文一

A：这件衣服很漂亮，您觉得怎么样？

B：不错，但是我想买一些特别的纪念品。

A：有什么想买的吗？

B：我想买一些当地手工艺品，
比如传统的刺绣或者瓷器。

A：那我们去附近的手工艺品店看看吧。

B：好的，我们去看看。

A：这里有一家不错的店铺，
他们有很多当地的特色产品。

B：太棒了！

kèwén yī

A：Zhè jiàn yīfu hěn piàoliang, nín juéde zěnmeyàng?

B：Búcuò, dànshì wǒ xiǎng mǎi yìxiē tèbié de jìniànpǐn.

A：Yǒu shénme xiǎng mǎide ma?

B：Wǒ xiǎng mǎi yìxiē dāngdì shǒugōngyìpǐn,

　　bǐrú chuántǒng de cìxiù huòzhě cíqì.

A：Nà wǒmen qù fùjìn de shǒugōngyìpǐn diàn kànkan ba.

B：Hǎo de, wǒmen qù kànkan.

A：Zhèlǐ yǒu yìjiā búcuò de diànpù,

    tāmen yǒu hěnduō dāngdì de tèsè chǎnpǐn.

B：Tài bàng le！

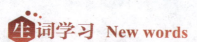 Exercises

一 **分角色朗读课文。** Role-play the conversation.

二 **根据课文内容，回答问题。** Answer questions according to the text.

  1. 这件衣服怎么样？

  2. B想买什么东西？

  3. 他们打算去哪里？

三 **听一听，跟读句子。** Listen and read the sentences.

  1. 您觉得怎么样？

  2. 我想买一些特别的纪念品。

  3. 我们去附近的手工艺品店看看吧。

  4. 我们去看看。

  5. 太棒了！

生词学习 New words

购物（动）	gòuwù	shopping
件（量）	jiàn	measurement of certain individual things, clothes, etc.
漂亮（形）	piàoliang	beautiful
一些（限定）	yīxiē	some
特别（形）	tèbié	special
纪念品（名）	jìniànpǐn	souvenir
当地（形）	dāngdì	local
手工艺品（名）	shǒugōngyìpǐn	handicrafts
比如（介）	bǐrú	often used to list things or give examples

传统（形）	chuántǒng	traditional
刺绣（名）	cìxiù	embroidery
瓷器（名）	cíqì	porcelain
附近（名）	fùjìn	nearby
店铺（名）	diànpù	shop
特色（形）	tèsè	the unique color, style, etc. that things exhibit
产品（名）	chǎnpǐn	product
棒（形）	bàng	awesome

 **课文 Texts**

课文二

（两人来到手工艺品店）

C：您好，欢迎光临！请问你们需要什么？

A：我们想看看你们店里有什么当地的特色产品。

C：当然，这里有很多传统的手工艺品。

B：这个茶具套装看起来很精美，
可以当作纪念品带回去。

C：是的，这个茶具套装是手工制作的，每个细节都非常用心。

A：好的，我们就买这个茶具套装吧。

C：好的，这个茶具套装是二百九十八元，
您需要刷卡还是付现金呢？

B：我们刷卡吧。

C：好的。感谢您的光临，祝您旅途愉快！

B：谢谢您，祝您生意兴隆！

kèwén èr

（Liǎng rén lái dào shǒugōngyìpǐn diàn）

C：Nín hǎo, huānyíng guānglín !

Qǐngwèn nǐmen xūyào shénme？

A：Wǒmen xiǎng kànkan nǐmen diàn lǐ yǒu shénme dāngdì de tèsè chǎnpǐn.

C：Dāngrán, zhèlǐ yǒu hěn duō chuántǒng de shǒugōngyìpǐn.

B：Zhège chájù tàozhuāng kànqǐlái hěn jīngměi,

　　kěyǐ dàngzuò jìniànpǐn dài huíqù.

C：Shì de, zhège chájù tàozhuāng shì shǒugōng zhìzuò de, měi gè xìjié dōu

　　fēicháng yòngxīn.

A：Hǎo de, wǒmen jiù mǎi zhège chájù tàozhuāng ba.

C：Hǎo de, zhège chájù tàozhuāng shì èrbǎijiǔshíbā yuán,

　　nín xūyào shuā kǎ háishì fù xiànjīn ne？

B：Wǒmen shuā kǎ ba.

C：Hǎo de. Gǎnxiè nín de guānglín, zhù nín lǚtú yúkuài！

B：Xièxie nín, zhù nín shēngyì xīnglóng！

课内练习 Exercises

一 **分角色朗读课文**。Role-play the conversation.

二 **根据课文内容，回答问题**。Answer questions according to the text.

　　1. 他们在哪里？

　　2. 他们买了什么？

　　3. 他们是怎么付钱的？

三 **听一听，跟读句子**。Listen and read the sentences.

　　1. 这个茶具套装看起来很精美。

　　2. 这个茶具套装是手工制作的。

　　3. 您需要刷卡还是付现金呢？

　　4. 祝您旅途愉快！

　　5. 祝您生意兴隆！

生词学习 New words

茶具（名）	chájù	tea set
套装（名）	tàozhuāng	refers to a set of things that are assembled together
精美（形）	jīngměi	exquisite
当作（动）	dàngzuò	taken as
带（动）	dài	bring
回去（动）	huíqù	back
手工（形）	shǒugōng	manual
制作（动）	zhìzuò	make
每（介）	měi	refers to any one or group within a specific range
细节（名）	xìjié	detail
用心（形）	yòngxīn	diligent
刷卡（动）	shuā kǎ	pay by cards
祝（动）	zhù	wish
旅途（名）	lǚtú	the journey
生意（名）	shēngyì	business
兴隆（形）	xīnglóng	prosperous

语言点链接 Language points

一 "觉得" 的用法 Usage of "觉得（juéde）"

"觉得" 是一个常见的动词，表示 "认为" "以为" "感觉" 等意思，常用于表达主观上的看法、意见或感受。

"觉得" is a common verb, refering to think, suppose, feel, etc. It is often used to express subjective views, opinions or feelings.

（1）她觉得这个人很有意思。

（2）你觉得我们现在该怎么办？

（3）他觉得自己需要更多的锻炼。

（4）我觉得今天的天气很好。

二 "比如"的用法 Usage of "比如（bǐrú）"

"比如"是一个常用的连词，用于引出具体的例子，起到举例说明的作用。

"比如" is a commonly used conjunction, which is used to introduce specific examples, serving the function of providing illustration.

（1）我喜欢吃各种水果，比如苹果、香蕉和橙子。

（2）旅游时要注意安全，比如不要走夜路、不要随意与陌生人交谈等。

（3）参加一些活动可以让生活更加有意义，比如音乐、运动、绘画等。

（4）职场中，你需要有一些必要的技能，比如沟通、协作和领导能力。

三 趋向补语的用法 Usage of 趋向补语（qūxiàng bǔyǔ）

趋向补语是汉语中的一类补语，用来表示动作的方向或趋向，可以修饰动词、形容词、副词等。它通常放在动词或形容词后面，用于表达动作或状态的方向或趋向。

Directional complement is one kind of complements in Chinese, which is used to indicate the direction or tendency of an action. It can modify verbs, adjectives, adverbs, etc. It is usually placed after a verb or adjective to express the direction or tendency of an action or state.

（1）他们拿走了我的行李。

（2）我哥打来了电话。

（3）气球慢慢地升起来了。

（4）这么好的东西，我要带回家去。

常用的复合趋向补语的引申用法：

The extended usages of commonly used compound directional complements:

v./adj.+ 起来	（1）她笑起来真好看。 （2）下雨了，衣服收起来！ （3）结婚后他就胖起来了。
v./adj.+ 出来	（1）这个办法是谁想出来的？ （2）我认出来了，你就是昨天帮助我的人。 （3）这个多出来的苹果就送给你吧。
v./adj.+ 下来	（1）从山上走下来花了我两小时。 （2）天暗下来了，我们快点儿回家吧。 （3）你停下来干嘛？这是绿灯。

v./adj.+ 下去	（1）你好，从这里走下去是不是有旅馆？ （2）只要你坚持下去，肯定能成功。 （3）再冷下去，我们得开暖气了。

一　"是……的"的用法 Usage of "是（shì）……的（de）"

以"是……的"为标记的动词谓语句，主要突出强调与动作相关的某个成分。"是"常出现在谓语动词前，有时出现在主语前；"的"常出现于句尾，个别时候出现在谓语动词后，宾语前。"是……的"中间一般多是短语结构。

A verb predicate sentence marked by "是……的" mainly emphasizes a certain element related to the action. "是" often appears before the predicate verb, and sometimes before the subject; "的" often appears at the end of the sentence, but occasionally it can be placed after the predicate verb and before the object. The structure between "是……的" is generally a phrase.

（1）我是坐飞机来的。

（2）这套茶具是用青瓷做的。

（3）这次旅行是我自己花钱的。

（4）这是我朋友买的水果，大家一起吃吧。

五　"每"的用法 Usage of "每（měi）"

"每"是代词，通常在量词之前，表示"各个"的意思，而且往往与其后的"都"搭配成句。

"每" is a pronoun that usually used before the measure word, expressing the meaning of "each", and it is often used in conjunction with the following "都" to form a sentence.

（1）每个人都很友好。

（2）这儿的每道菜都好吃。

（3）每个地方都有自己的特色。

（4）他会准备好每次旅行的物品。

六　"祝"的用法 Usage of "祝（zhù）"

"祝"是一个表示祝福、祝愿的汉字。它通常用于表达对他人的美好愿望和祝福，是一种礼貌和尊重的表达方式。

"祝" is a Chinese character that expresses blessing and best wishes. It is typically used to convey good wishes and blessings to others, serving as a polite and respectful way of expressing one's hopes for someone's well-being.

（1）祝你生日快乐。

（2）祝你考试成功。

（3）祝你身体健康。

（4）祝你们新婚快乐，百年好合。

课后练习 Exercises

一 看拼音写汉字。 Look at the pinyin and write the words.

dāng dì	huò zhě	fù jìn	tè sè	chǎn pǐn
（　　）	（　　）	（　　）	（　　）	（　　）

dàng zuò	shǒu gōng	zhì zuò	xì jié	lǚ tú
（　　）	（　　）	（　　）	（　　）	（　　）

二 选词填空。 Choose the correct word to fill in the blanks.

兴隆	愉快	精美	传统	用心

1. 这家餐厅的菜品不仅美味，而且摆盘非常（　　　）。

2. 她每天都会（　　　）准备自己的工作。

3. 我们一家人在海边度过了一个（　　　）的假期。

4. 祝您的生意（　　　），越来越红火。

5. 这家酒店采用（　　　）的建筑风格，非常有特色。

三 对话配对。 Match the sentences.

1	祝你旅途愉快。		A	太大了！
2	这里有一家不错的店铺。		B	刷卡吧。
3	有什么想吃的吗？		C	我们去看看。
4	你觉得怎么样？		D	让我想想。
5	刷卡还是付现金？		E	谢谢！

四 填写正确的补语完成句子。 Fill in the correct complement to complete the sentence.

1. 你的新衣服看（　　　）很漂亮。

2. 这本书可以带（　　　）吗？

3. 走（　　　）的那个人是你朋友吗？

4. 这个菜看（　　　）不怎么样，吃（　　　）很不错啊！

5. 我妈说我买（　　　）的东西很用心。

五 **听录音，判断对错。**Listen to the recording and judge whether the statements are correct or incorrect.

1. 我很喜欢喝茶。　　　　　　　　　□

2. 我的朋友喜欢买茶叶。　　　　　　□

3. 我送给她的生日礼物是一套茶具。　□

旅游小贴士 **Travel Tips**

货币[1]

一 中国货币

中国的货币叫作人民币，是由国家银行中国人民银行发行的。人民币的单位是元，辅币是角和分。一元为十角，一角为十分。元、角和分有纸币，元和五角及分也有铸币。元的票面有 1 元、2 元、5 元、10 元、20 元、50 元、100 元，角的票面有 1 角、5 角，分的票面有 1 分、2 分、5 分。人民币元的缩写符号是 RMB￥。

二 外币兑换

我国现在可以收兑的外币有：

英镑、港币、美元、瑞士法郎、新加坡元、瑞典克朗、挪威克朗、日元、丹麦克朗、加拿大元、澳大利亚元、欧元、菲律宾比索、泰国铢、韩国元等。银行办理外币的兑入和兑出业务，称为外币兑换业务。

根据我国现行的外汇管理法令规定，在中华人民共和国境内，禁止外币流通，并且不得以外币计价结算。为了方便来华旅游的外宾，以及港澳台同胞用款，中国银行及其他外汇指定银行除受理外币旅行支票、外国信用卡兑换人民

1　详见：https://www.gov.cn/banshi/2005-05/31/content_2574.htm.

币的业务外，还受理 22 种外币现钞，以及台湾新台币的兑换业务。另外，为了尽量对持兑人给予方便，除了银行以外，一些宾馆、饭店或商店也可办理外币兑换人民币的业务。兑换后未用完的人民币在离境前可凭 6 个月内有效期内的外汇兑换单兑换成外币，携带出境。不同情况兑换时使用不同的牌价。兑换旅行支票、信用卡、汇款使用买入价；兑出外汇，包括兑出外币现钞，使用卖出汇价；兑入外币现钞，使用现钞买入价。

三 在中国代办的外国信用卡

目前，可在中国代办的外国信用卡主要有：

万事达卡（MasterCard）、

维萨卡（Visa Card）、

运通卡（American Express Card）、

JCB 卡（JCBCard）、

大莱卡（Diners Club Card）。

Currency

Chinese Currency

The currency of China is called Renminbi (RMB), issued by the People's Bank of China, the national bank. The unit of RMB is the Yuan, with the subsidiary units being the Jiao and the Fen. One Yuan equals ten Jiao, and one Jiao equals ten Fen. Yuan, Jiao, and Fen are available in banknotes, while Yuan, five-Jiao, and Fen are also available in minted coins. The denominations of Yuan notes include 1, 2, 5, 10, 20, 50, and 100 Yuan. The denominations of Jiao paper money are 1, 2, and 5 Jiao, and Fen coins are available in denominations of 1, 2, and 5 Fen. The abbreviation symbol for Chinese Yuan is RMB ￥.

Foreign Currency Exchange

The foreign currencies currently accepted for exchange in China include:

British Pound, US Dollar, Swiss Franc, Singapore Dollar, Swedish Krona, Norwegian Krona, Japanese Yen, Danish Krone, Canadian Dollar, Australian Dollar,

Euro, Philippine Peso, Thai Baht, South Korean Won, etc. Banks handle the exchange of foreign currencies, both buying and selling, which constitutes foreign currency exchange services.

According to China's current foreign exchange regulations, the circulation of foreign currencies is prohibited within the territory of the People's Republic of China, and transactions cannot be settled in foreign currency. To facilitate the spending needs of foreign visitors, and compatriots from Hong Kong, Macau, and Taiwan, the Bank of China and other designated foreign exchange banks accept foreign travelers' checks and foreign credit cards for exchange into Renminbi. They also handle the exchange of 22 foreign currency notes and New Taiwan Dollars. Moreover, to provide greater convenience, some hotels, restaurants, or stores may also offer foreign currency exchange services. Unused Renminbi can be exchanged back into foreign currencies before departure with a valid foreign exchange receipt within six months. Different exchange rates apply to different scenarios: the buying rate is used for traveler's checks, credit cards, and remittances; the selling rate is used for foreign currency outflow, including foreign currency notes; and the buying rate for cash applies to foreign currency notes.

Foreign Credit Cards Accepted in China

Currently, the major foreign credit cards that can be processed in China include: MasterCard, Visa Card, American Express Card, JCB Card, Diners Club Card.

第五单元

应急

Unit 5
Emergency Response

在本单元，你会进入一些特殊的场景。你会了解到迷路的时候可以怎么向他人求助，如何在丢失物品的时候进行处理以及如何在中国就医等相关内容的表达，这些都能够帮助你更好地解决在中国旅行时遇到的问题。

In this unit, you will encounter some special scenarios. You will learn how to seek help from others when you get lost, how to handle situations when you lose something, and how to seek medical treatment in China, among other related expressions. All of these can help you better solve the problems you encounter while traveling in China.

第十三课
Lesson 13 迷 路
Get Lost

课前热身 Warm up

1. 如果你到一个陌生的地方旅游，你会通过什么方式找到你想去的地方呢？

2. 如果你迷路了，你会怎么办呢？

课文 Texts

课文一

A：对不起，打扰一下。

我迷路了，您能告诉我怎么去这个地方吗？

B：我看一下，您是要去这里的博物馆吗？

A：是的，是的。您能告诉我怎么去吗？

B：我也要去那个方向。让我带您过去吧！

A：太谢谢您了！这里离博物馆远吗？

B：不远，走路的话十分钟就到了。

A：到了，博物馆就在银行旁边。

您过马路吧，我先走了。

B：太感谢了！再见！

kèwén yī

A：Duìbuqǐ, dǎrǎo yíxià.

Wǒ mílù le, nín néng gàosu wǒ zěnme qù zhègè dìfang ma?

B：Wǒ kàn yíxià, nín shì yào qù zhèlǐ de bówùguǎn ma?

A：Shì de, shì de. Nín néng gàosu wǒ zěnme qù ma?

B：Wǒ yě yào qù nàge fāngxiàng. Ràng wǒ dài nín guòqù ba !

A：Tài Xièxie nín le! Zhèlǐ lí bówùguǎn yuǎn ma?

B：Bù yuǎn, zǒulù de huà shí fēnzhōng jiù dào le.

A：Dào le, bówùguǎn jiù zài yínháng pángbiān.

　　Nín guò mǎlù ba, wǒ xiān zǒu le.

B：Tài gǎnxiè le! Zàijiàn!

课内练习 Exercises

一 **分角色朗读课文**。Role-play the conversation.

二 **根据课文内容，回答问题**。Answer questions according to the text.

　　1. A怎么了？

　　2. A要去哪儿？

　　3. B告诉A怎么走了吗？

　　4. A要去的地方远吗？

　　5. A要去的地方在哪儿？

三 **听一听，跟读句子**。Listen and read the sentences.

　　1. 对不起，打扰一下。

　　2. 您能告诉我怎么去这个地方吗？

　　3. 让我带您过去吧。

　　4. 这里离博物馆远吗？

　　5. 您过马路吧，我先走了。

生词学习 New words

打扰（动）	dǎrǎo	disturb
迷路（动）	mílù	get lost
地方（名）	dìfang	place
博物馆（名）	bówùguǎn	museum
方向（名）	fāngxiàng	direction
让（介）	ràng	let
走路（动）	zǒulù	walk

旁边（名）	pángbiān	side
过（动）	guò	cross
马路（名）	mǎlù	road

课文 Texts

A：对不起，打扰一下。

　　您能告诉我我现在在地图上的什么地方吗？

B：我看一下，我们在这里，您要去哪里？

A：我可能迷路了，我想去火车站。从这里可以到火车站吗？

B：我想一下。您可以在这里坐地铁去火车站。

　　先坐一号线到鼓楼，然后换乘二号线到火车站。

A：太谢谢您了！我可以去哪里坐地铁？

B：这条路一直往前走到十字路口，然后往右转，

　　再直走，您就能看见地铁站了。

A：太好了，谢谢您。

B：不客气！再见！

kèwén èr

A：Duìbuqǐ, dǎrǎo yíxià.

　　Nín néng gàosù wǒ wǒ xiànzài zài dìtú shàng de shénme dìfang ma?

B：Wǒ kàn yíxià, wǒmen zài zhèlǐ, nín yào qù nǎlǐ?

A：Wǒ kěnéng mílù le, wǒ xiǎng qù huǒchēzhàn.

　　Cóng zhèlǐ kěyǐ dào huǒchēzhàn ma?

B：Wǒ xiǎng yíxià. Nín kěyǐ zài zhèlǐ zuò dìtiě qù huǒchēzhàn.

　　Xiān zuò yī hào xiàn dào Gǔlóu,

　　ránhòu huànchéng èr hào xiàn dào huǒchēzhàn.

A：Tài Xièxie nín le! Wǒ kěyǐ qù nǎlǐ zuò dìtiě?

B：Zhè tiáo lù yìzhí wǎng qián zǒu dào shízì lùkǒu,

ránhòu wǎng yòu zhuǎn, zài zhí zǒu, nǐn jiù néng kànjiàn dìtiě zhàn le.

A: Tài hǎo le, Xièxie nín.

B: Bukèqi! Zàijiàn!

内练习　Exercises

一　分角色朗读课文。Role-play the conversation.

二　根据课文内容，回答问题。Answer questions according to the text.

　　1. A想去哪里？

　　2. A可以坐地铁去吗？

　　3. A可以坐几号线？

　　4. A知道去哪里坐地铁吗？

　　5. 可以怎么去地铁站呢？

三　听一听，跟读句子。Listen and read the sentences.

　　1. 您能告诉我我现在在地图上的什么地方吗？

　　2. 我可能迷路了，我想去火车站。

　　3. 先坐一号线到鼓楼，然后换乘二号线到火车站。

　　4. 我可以去哪里坐地铁？

　　5. 从这儿一直往前走到十字路口。

生词学习　New words

地图（名）	dìtú	map
线（名）	xiàn	line
换乘（动）	huànchéng	transfer
条（量）	tiáo	measure word used for long and thin things
一直（副）	yīzhí	straight
往（介）	wǎng	to, towards
十字（名）	shízì	cross

路口（名）	lùkǒu	junction
转（动）	zhuǎn	turn
看见（动）	kànjiàn	see

语言点链接 Language points

一 "想"的用法 Usage of "想（xiǎng）"

"想"是一个能愿动词，表示希望、打算，用在其他动词或者动词短语前面。用来表达某人希望做什么事情。

否定形式是在前面加"不"，构成"不想"。

"想" is a modal verb, indicating desire or intention. It is used before a verb or a verb phrase to express that someone wants to do something.

The negative form is to add a preceding "不", forming "不想".

（1）我想去北京玩一下。

（2）我想吃面条，不想吃汉堡包。

（3）你想去哪儿？

二 "离"的用法 Usage of "离（lí）"

"离"可以用来表示在时间或空间上的距离，基本结构为"A离B……"，在一些语境里，"A"可以省略，变成"离B……"。

"离" can be used to represent the distance in time or space, with the basic structure of "A离B……". In some contexts, "A" can be omitted, becoming "离B……".

（1）宁波离上海不太远。

（2）（今天）离她的生日只有2天了。

（3）（现在）离出发还有1个小时。

三 "……的话，……" Usage of "……的话（dehuà），……"

"……的话，……"常常用于口语中，用来表示假设。它的完整形式是"要是……的话，……"。

"……的话，……" is often used in spoken Chinese, indicating a supposition. It's an abbreviated form of "要是……的话，……".

（1）（要是）你有空的话，就过来我这里玩吧。

（2）（要是）你有时间的话，我们就可以一起去旅游。

（3）（要是）下午不下雨的话，我就去跑步。

四 量词"条"的用法 Usage of measure word "条（tiáo）"

量词"条"可以用于不同的事物，主要用来描述细长的事物，也可以用来描述与人有关的事物。

The measure word "条" can be used for different things, mainly to describe long and thin things, and can also be used to describe things related to people.

（1）细长的事物 long and thin things

一条马路、一条小河、一条蛇、一条裤子

（2）与人有关的 things related to people

一条腿、一条心、一条性命

五 介词"往"的用法 Usage of preposition "往（wǎng）"

在指示方向的时候，常常需要用到介词"往"加上方位词。

When indicating direction, it is common to use the preposition "往" combined with directional words.

（1）先走 5 分钟，然后往右转，就是地铁站了。

（2）先直走然后往左走，就能看到医院了。

（3）一直往前走就能看到了。

六 兼语句的用法 Usage of 兼语句（jiānyǔ jù）

兼语句的谓语部分通常是由一个动宾短语和一个主谓短语组成，前一个动宾短语的宾语兼做后面主谓短语的主语，所以称为兼语句。兼语句的第一个动词往往是使令动词，如"请""让""叫"等。

The predicate part of a Bi-constituent sentence is usually composed of a verb-object phrase and a subject-predicate phrase, with the object of the previous verb-object phrase serving as the subject of the subsequent subject-predicate phrase, hence it is called a Bi-constituent sentence. The first verb in a Bi-constituent sentence is often a causative verb, such as "请" (to invite), "让" (to let) and "叫" (to ask).

（1）导游让我们明天早上 9 点集合（gathering）。

（2）妈妈叫我去超市买一些苹果。

（3）我想请你帮我修一下电脑。

课后练习 Exercises

一 看拼音写汉字。Look at the pinyin and write the words.

mí lù	gào su	zǒu lù	páng biān	lù kǒu
（　　　）	（　　　）	（　　　）	（　　　）	（　　　）

zhuǎn	kàn jiàn	dì fang	mǎ lù	bówù guǎn
（　　　）	（　　　）	（　　　）	（　　　）	（　　　）

二 选词填空。Choose the correct word to fill in the blanks.

迷路	再	一直	换乘	往

1. 我今天先不去了，明天（　　　）去。

2. 我好像（　　　）了，还没找到博物馆。

3. 去博物馆需要（　　　）地铁。

4. （　　　）左走 100 米就到博物馆了。

5. 我今天有点累。因为（　　　）在走路。

三 改写句子。Rewrite the sentences.

例如：老师说："同学们，请打开摄像头。"
　　　老师让同学们打开摄像头。

1. 爸爸对我说："帮我修一下电脑。"

　　_____

2. 检票员对她说："请出示您的护照。"

　　_____

3. 姐姐对我说："你跟我一起去上海吧。"

　　_____

4. 妈妈对我说："赶紧去洗澡。"

　　_____

四 替换画线部分。Replace the underline parts with the given words or phrases.

1. 您能告诉我怎么<u>去这个地方</u>吗？

①去火车站吗　　　　②买火车票吗　　　　③写这个汉字吗

　　_____

2. 这里的风景太美了。

①这里的交通/方便　　　　　②汉字/难写　　　　　③这件衣服/贵

---

3. 走路的话，十分钟就能到。

①方便/就帮我订一下机票　　　②你去/我就跟你一起去

③不忙/我们一起去看电影吧

---

4. 明天我想去游乐园玩。

①下午/去超市买水果　　　　　②后天/买一些礼物给妈妈

③下周/去上海

---

5. 我家离机场不远。

①杭州/上海很近　　　　　　　②现在/过年很远

③现在/商场关门只有 10 分钟了

五　把下面的词语整理成句子。Rearrange the following words and phrases to make sentences.

1. 您　　告诉　　怎么　　医院　　能　　吗　　我　　去

2. 让　　带　　吧　　您　　过去　　我

3. 医院　　左边　　就　　学校　　在

4. 沿着　　往　　走　　前　　这　　条　　路

5. 您　　坐　　机场　　地铁　　去　　可以

六　听录音，判断对错。Listen to the recording and judge whether the statements are correct or incorrect.

1. 女生想去机场。　　　　　　☐

2. 女生只能坐地铁去那里。　　☐

3. 去机场需要换乘地铁。　　　☐

4. 地铁站就在前面不远。　　　□

5. 到路口后往左转就到地铁站了。　□

旅游小贴士　Travel Tips

如何在旅行时避免迷路？

　　当我们在中国旅行，尤其是自由行的时候，很可能会遇到迷路的情况。在异国的街头，听着陌生的语言，会给我们造成很大的不便。那我们要怎么尽可能减少这种情况的发生呢？

一　提前了解当地环境和旅游信息

　　在旅行前，应该提前了解当地的环境和旅游信息，包括当地的交通、景点、气候等方面的信息。这样可以帮助旅行者更好地了解当地的情况，制订合理的旅游计划，减少迷路和失踪的风险。

二　选择可靠的旅游机构和导游

　　选择可靠的旅游机构和导游也是预防迷路和失踪的重要措施之一。旅行者应该选择正规的旅行社或导游，并了解其资质和信誉情况。在旅游过程中，应该听从导游的安排和指示，不要擅自离开团队或改变行程。

三　携带必要的旅游安全装备

　　旅行者应该携带必要的旅游安全装备，如手机、充电器、地图、指南针等。这些装备可以帮助旅行者在需要时与他人联系、获取帮助或找到正确的方向。此外，还可以携带一些必要的药品和急救用品，以应对紧急情况。

四 注意个人安全和自我保护

　　个人安全和自我保护是预防迷路和失踪的重要措施之一。旅行者应该时刻保持警觉，注意周围的环境和人群，避免到危险的地方游览或探险。在旅游过程中，应该注意自己的随身物品和贵重物品的安全，避免被盗或遗失。

五 与家人或朋友保持联系

　　在旅游过程中，与家人或朋友保持联系是非常重要的。旅行者应该提前告知家人或朋友自己的行程和计划，并保持联系。在旅游过程中，可以通过电话、短信等方式与家人或朋友保持联系，让他们知道自己的行踪和情况。

六 积极配合当地警方和旅游机构的工作

　　在旅游过程中，如果发生迷路或失踪的情况，应该积极配合当地警方和旅游机构的工作。如向当地警方报案并协助调查，向旅游机构报告情况并寻求帮助。同时，也可以向其他旅行者或当地居民寻求帮助，让他们提供指导和支持。

七 学习一些基本的当地语言和沟通技巧

　　在旅游过程中，学习一些基本的当地语言和沟通技巧也是非常有帮助的。这些技巧可以帮助旅行者更好地与当地人交流和沟通，获取更多的信息和帮助。同时，也可以减少因语言障碍而发生迷路或失踪的风险。

How to avoid getting lost while traveling?

When we travel in China, especially on a independent tour, getting lost can be a common issue. Listening to an unfamiliar language on the streets of a foreign country can create great inconveniences. How can we minimize the occurrence of this situation as much as possible?

1. Familiarize yourself with the local environment and tourism information

Before traveling, it is important to research the local environment and tourism information in advance, including information on local transportation, attractions, climate, and other aspects. This can help travelers better understand the local situation, plan their trips wisely, and reduce the risk of getting lost and missing.

2. Choose reliable travel agencies and guides

Choosing a reliable travel agency and guide is also one of the important measures to prevent getting lost or missing. Travelers should choose a reputable travel agency or tour guide and check their qualifications and reputation. During the trip, follow the guide's arrangements and instructions and avoid leaving the group or changing the itinerary on your own.

3. Carry necessary travel safety equipment

Travelers should carry necessary travel safety equipment, such as mobile phones, chargers, maps, compasses, etc. These items can help travelers connect with others, get help, or find the right direction when needed. In addition, carrying some basic medicines and first aid supplies is also advisable to cope with emergencies.

4. Pay attention to personal safety and self-protection

Personal safety and self-protection are crucial measures to prevent getting lost and missing. Travelers should stay alert, pay attention to the surroundings and people around them, and avoid visiting or exploring dangerous areas. Keep an eye on personal belongings and valuable items to avoid theft or loss.

5. Stay in touch with family or friends

It is very important to maintain contact with family or friends during the travel. Travelers should inform their family or friends of their itinerary and plans in advance and keep in touch. During the travel process, use phone calls, text messages, and other means to update them on your whereabouts and situation.

6. Actively cooperate with local authorities and tourism agencies

If there is a situation of getting lost or missing, actively cooperate with the local police and tourism agencies. Report the case to the local police and assist with their investigation, and notify the tourism agency to seek help. At the same time, you can also seek guidance and support from other travelers or local residents.

7. Learn some basic local languages and communication skills

Learning some basic local languages and communication skills is also very helpful. These skills can help travelers better communicate and interact with locals, allowing you to obtain more information and assistance. It can also reduce the risk of getting lost or missing due to language barriers.

课前热身 Warm up

1. 旅行的时候你有丢失过物品吗？

2. 你是怎么找回丢失的物品的？

课文 Texts

课文一

A：您好，先生！有什么可以帮您？

B：您好，我找不到我的行李了。

A：您先别着急，慢慢说。您丢了几件行李？

B：就一件。我刚才在咖啡厅喝咖啡，把行李放在桌子下面了。
我喝完咖啡后，行李箱就不见了。

A：您丢的是怎么样的行李箱？

B：是一个很小的棕色的皮箱，上面有我的姓名贴。

A：可能是有人拿错了。
您把您的姓名和联系方式留给我，我们会尽量给您找。

B：好的，需要多久呢？

A：对不起，现在我也不知道。
您看这样行吗？
您先回去，我们一有消息就通知您。

B：好的，谢谢。

kèwén yī

A：Nín hǎo, xiānsheng! Yǒu shénme kěyǐ bāng nín?

B：Nín hǎo, wǒ zhǎo bú dào wǒ de xíngli le.

A：Nín xiān bié zháojí, mànmàn shuō. Nín diūle jǐ jiàn xíngli?

B：Jiù yí jiàn.

Wǒ gāngcái zài kāfēi tīng hē kāfēi, bǎ xíngli fàng zài zhuōzi xiàmiàn le.

Wǒ hē wán kāfēi hòu, xíngli xiāng jiù bú jiàn le.

A：Nín diū de shì zěnme yàng de xíngli xiāng?

B：Shì yí gè hěn xiǎo de zōngsè de píxiāng, shàngmiàn yǒu wǒ de xìngmíng tiē.

A：Kěnéng shì yǒu rén nácuòle.

Nín bǎ nín de xìngmíng hé liánxì fāngshì liú gěi wǒ, wǒmen huì jǐnliàng gěi nín zhǎo.

B：Hǎo de, xūyào duō jiǔ ne?

A：Duìbuqǐ, xiànzài wǒ yě bù zhīdào.

Nín kàn zhèyang xíng ma?

Nín xiān huíqù, wǒmen yì yǒu xiāoxi jiù tōngzhī nín.

B：Hǎo de, Xièxie.

课内练习 Exercises

一 分角色朗读课文。Role-play the conversation.

二 根据课文内容，回答问题。Answer questions according to the text.

1. B怎么了？

2. B的行李放在哪了？

3. B的行李是怎么样的？

4. 行李可能怎么了？

5. 找行李需要多久？

三 听一听，跟读句子。Listen and read the sentences.

1. 有什么可以帮您？

2. 我找不到我的行李了。

3. 您先别着急，慢慢说。

4. 我把行李放在桌子下面了。

5. 我们一有消息就通知您。

生词学习 New words

行李（名）	xíngli	luggage
丢（动）	diū	lose
刚才（副）	gāngcái	just now
箱（名）	xiāng	case
棕色（名）	zōngsè	brown
贴（名）	tiē	sticker
方式（名）	fāngshì	way, method
留（动）	liú	leave
尽量（副）	jǐnliàng	try one's best
消息（名）	xiāoxi	message
通知（动）	tōngzhī	inform, notify

课文 Texts

A：您好，有什么可以帮助您?

B：您好，我来取之前丢失的行李箱。

A：好的，您先请坐。请您出示一下您的身份证，可以吗?

B：当然可以，给您。

A：好的，请您告诉我您的行李箱是什么样子的。

B：一个棕色的小行李箱，上面贴着我的名字。

A：好的，我确信这是您的行李箱。您可以拿走了。

B：你们非常负责，也非常热心，谢谢你们!

A：您太客气了!

kèwén èr

A：Nín hǎo, yǒu shénme kěyǐ bāngzhù nín?

B：Nín hǎo, wǒ lái qǔ zhīqián diūshī de xíngli xiāng.

A：Hǎo de, nín xiān qǐng zuò.

　　Qǐng nín chūshì yíxià nín de shēnfènzhèng, kěyǐ ma?

B：Dāngrán kěyǐ, gěi nín.

A：Hǎo de, qǐng nín gàosù wǒ nín de xíngli xiāng shì shénme yàngzi de.

B：Yí gè zōngsè de xiǎo xíngli xiāng, shàngmiàn yǒu tiēzhe wǒ de míngzì.

A：Hǎo de, wǒ quèxìn zhè shì nín de xíngli xiāng. Nín kěyǐ názǒule.

B：Nǐmen fēicháng fùzé, yě fēicháng rèxīn, Xièxie nǐmen!

A：Nín tài kèqi le !

课内练习 Exercises

一 **分角色朗读课文**。Role-play the conversation.

二 **根据课文内容，回答问题**。Answer questions according to the text.

　　1. B来做什么？

　　2. A请B出示什么？

　　3. 行李箱是B的吗？

　　4. B觉得工作人员怎么样？

三 **听一听，跟读句子**。Listen and read the sentences.

　　1. 您好，有什么可以帮助您？

　　2. 请您出示一下您的身份证，可以吗？

　　3. 请您告诉我您的行李箱是什么样子的。

　　4. 您可以拿走了。

　　5. 你们非常负责，也非常热心。

生词学习 New words

帮助（动）	bāngzhù	help
之前（副）	zhīqián	previous
丢失（动）	diūshī	lose
样子（名）	yàngzi	appearance, shape
负责（形）	fùzé	responsible
热心（形）	rèxīn	kind-hearted

语言点链接 Language points

◯ "别+v."的用法 Usage of "别（bié）+v."

1. "别"放在动词前，常常用来表示劝阻或禁止，相当于"不要"。

When "别" is used before a verb, it often means to give advice or commands to other people, the meaning of which is same as不要.

（1）别着急。

（2）别担心。

（3）别在旅游景点买东西，太贵了。

2. 在"别+v."后面加"了"，构成"别+v.+了"表示阻止或禁止别人正在做的事情。

When "别+v." is added with 了 after it to form "别+v.+了", it means preventing or prohibiting someone from continuing an action they are currently doing.

(1) 别玩手机了，明天要早起。

(2) 别睡了，我们出去走一走吧。

(3) 别吃了，吃太多会不舒服的。

◯ "v.+得/不"的用法 Usage of "v.+得/不（de/bù）"

"v.+得/不+结果补语/趋向补语"常常用来表示可能性。动词后面用"得/不"引出有没有条件或可能有某种结果或趋向。它的否定形式用得较多，肯定形式主要用于回答疑问句和反问句。

"v.+得/不+resultative/directional complement" is usually used to indicate the possibility. After the verb,得/不 is used to introduce whether there are conditions or

possible outcomes or tendencies. Its negative form is used more frequently, while the affirmative form is mainly used to answer questions and rhetorical questions.

肯定形式	v.＋得＋结果补语 / 趋向补语 (+O)。		我听得懂中文。
否定形式	v.＋不＋结果补语 / 趋向补语 (+O)。		我听不懂中文。
疑问句	肯定形式＋否定形式 (+O)		你听得懂听不懂中文？
	肯定形式 (+O) ＋吗？		你听得懂中文吗？

（1）我找不到我的行李了。

（2）A：我说话，你们听得见吗？

B：刚才听不见，现在听得见了。

三 "处所+v.+着+n." 的用法 Usage of "处所（chùsuǒ）+v.＋着（zhe）+n."

"处所+v.+着+n." 可以用来表示存在。

"location+v.+着+n." can be used to indicate existence.

（1）上面贴着我的名字。

（2）墙上贴着一张海报。

（3）门口停着一辆大巴车。

（4）她手上拿着很多东西。

（5）桌子上放着一本书。

四 "一……就……" 的用法 Usage of "一（yī）……就（jiù）……"

"一……就……" 分别连接两个动作，表示"就……"后面的动作紧接着"一……"的动作发生。

"一……就……" connect two actions separately, indicating that the action following "就……" occurs immediately after the action following "一……".

（1）我们一有消息就通知您。

（2）雨一停，我们就出发。

（3）她一回家就洗澡。

（4）我想一放假就去上海玩。

五 "把" 字句的用法 Usage of "把（bǎ）sentence"

1. "把" 字句第一种的基本结构为 "S+把+O+v.+在/到/给+其他成分"，表示主语 S 通过某一个动作 v. 把宾语 O 的位置移动到另一个地方（其他成分）。

The first basic structure of "把 sentence" 1 is "S+把+O+v.+在/到/给+other components"，indicating that the subject S moves the position of object O to another place (other components) through an action v.

S	P				
	把	O	v.	在 / 到 / 给	
我	把	您	送	到	机场。
请你	把	包	放	在	桌子上。
我	把	行李箱	放	在	桌子下面了。
您	把	您的姓名和联系方式	留	给	我。

2. "把"字句的第二种基本结构为"S+把+O+v.+补语"，表示主语S通过某一个动作v.使宾语O发生了变化，产生了某一种结果。

The second basic structure of "把 sentence" is "S+把+O+v.+complement", which means that the subject S changes the object O through an action v. and produces a certain result.

S	P			
	把	O	v.	补语
我	把	客人	送	走了。
她	把	会议室	准备	好了。
我	把	办公室	打扫	干净了。
我	把	PPT	做	好了。

课后练习 Exercises

一 看拼音写汉字。Look at the pinyin and write the words.

xíng li　　　zháo jí　　　lián xì　　　jǐn liàng　　　tōng zhī

(　　　)　　(　　　)　　(　　　)　　(　　　)　　(　　　)

diū shī　　　gāng cái　　　fù zé　　　rè xīn　　　bāng zhù

(　　　)　　(　　　)　　(　　　)　　(　　　)　　(　　　)

二 选词填空。Choose the correct word to fill in the blanks.

别	丢	贴	尽量	留

1. 今天太晚了，你（　　　）走了。

2. 请把这张海报（　　　）到墙上。

3. 听说他昨天把手机（　　　）了。

4. 老师给我们（　　　）了很多作业。

5. 最近我们都很忙，我（　　　）在周五完成这个项目。

三 改写句子。Rewrite the sentences.

例如：他看得懂中文小说。

　　　他看得懂中文小说吗？

　　　他看不懂中文小说。

1. 我看得见海报上的字。

_____

2. 我听得懂中国人说话。

_____

3. 我听得清楚你说的话。

_____

4. 他今天做得完作业。

_____

四 替换画线部分。Replace the underline parts with the given words or phrases.

1. 行李箱上面 贴着我的名字。

①房间里/坐/很多客人　　　　　②沙发上/堆/很多衣服

③文件袋里/装/一些证件

_____

2. 我们一有消息就通知您。

①我们/到周末/去爬山。　　　　②今天工作/结束/去打篮球

③我/放假/回家

_____

3. 我把手机放在包里了。

①我/衣服放在沙发上了。　　　　②请/水放在桌子上。

③你/她的微信号发给我吧。

五 把下面的词语整理成句子。Rearrange the following words and phrases to make sentences.

1. 我　　之前　　来　　的　　丢失　　取　　手机

2. 我　　手机　　的　　找　　了　　不到　　我

3. 请　　有　　通知　　一　　就　　消息　　您　　我

4. 您　　姓名　　留　　把　　电话　　我　　给　　和

5. 写　　上面　　时间　　起飞　　的　　着

六 听录音，判断对错。Listen to the recording and judge whether the statements are correct or incorrect.

1. 这段对话发生在机场。　☐

2. 这位女士丢了手机。　☐

3. 手机是在打车的时候丢的。　☐

4. 这是一个紫色的手机。　☐

5. 工作人员帮这位女士找到了手机。　☐

旅游小贴士 Travel Tips

铁路出行中丢失物品怎么办？[1]

在中国旅行的时候，铁路出行将会是我们首选的出行方式。在旅行中丢失物品是一件影响行程和心情的事情。那在遇到这种情况，我们可以做些什么呢？

（1）拨打铁路客服电话 12306，按照客服工作人员提示，提供遗失物品的详细特征，如种类、外观、颜色和尺寸等信息，客服工作人员会根据信息，联系相关单位进行查找。

（2）登录铁路 12306 App 或官网。在手机上打开 12306 App，点击首页"温

1　详见：http://news.cnr.cn/native/gd/20231014/t20231014_526450901.shtml.

馨服务",或者点击"我的"页面,选择"遗失物品",点击"遗失物品查找",按照要求提交相关信息。

（3）向工作人员寻求帮助。无论您在列车上还是车站里,都可以求助工作人员。遗失物品找回后,铁路工作人员会与您联系。您只需要提供联系方式,领取车站等信息,即可前往车站服务台或遗失物品招领处查询领取。已经乘车离开的旅客也无需担心,工作人员会根据您的需求,将遗失物品转送至列车可以到达的指定车站。

（4）领取失物。本人领取时需携带有效身份证件,提供乘车信息。也可以请人代领,代领人领取时需携带有效身份证件,以及失主的委托书和失主的有效身份证件复印件,并提供乘车信息。

What should we do if we lose something while traveling by train?

When traveling in China, railway transportation will be our preferred mode of transportation. Losing items during a trip is a common yet frustrating occurrence that can affect both your schedule and mood. What can we do when encountering such a situation?

（1）Call the national railway customer service hotline 12306 and follow the voice prompts to switch to manual service. According to the customer service staff's prompts, provide detailed characteristics of the lost item, such as type, appearance, color, and size information. The customer service staff will contact relevant units to search based on the information.

（2）Log in to the official website of Railway 12306, www.12306. cn or open 12306 App on your mobile device, tap "Warm Service" on the homepage, or go to the "My" page and select "Lost Items", then click on " Search for Lost Items". and submit the relevant information as required.

（3）Seek help from the staff. Whether you are on the train or at the station, you can seek help from the on-site staff. After the lost item is found, the railway staff will contact you. You only need to provide your contact information, station information that you want to get your items back, etc., Passengers who have already left by train do not need to worry. The staff will transfer the lost items to the designated station that the train can reach according to your needs.

（4）Retrieve lost items. You need to bring a valid identification document and provide information about the lost items. You can also ask someone to collect it on your behalf. When collecting on your behalf, he or she may need to bring his or her valid ID card, as well as the owner's power of attorney and a copy of the owner's valid ID card, and provide your travel information.

第十五课
Lesson 15 就 医
See A Doctor

 前热身 **Warm up**

1. 旅行的时候你有身体不舒服的时候吗？

2. 你是怎么处理的？

 文 **Texts**

课文一

A：沙地，你怎么还没起床？我们不是说好今天去博物馆的吗？

B：我有点儿不舒服，头有点儿疼。

A：你是不是感冒了？

B：可能是。昨天不是下雨了吗？我没带伞，被雨淋了。

A：那我们去看一下医生吧？

B：先不用了，我想先睡一会，睡醒可能就好了。

A：行吧，你先休息。

下午如果还不舒服，我们就去看医生。

B：好的，不好意思，今天不能去博物馆了。

A：没关系，身体要紧！

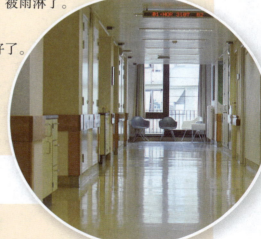

kèwén yī

A：Shādì, nǐ zěnme hái méi qǐchuáng?

Wǒmen búshì shuōhǎo jīntiān qù bówùguǎn de ma?

B：Wǒ yǒudiǎnr bù shūfu, tóu yǒudiǎnr téng.

A：Nǐ shì búshì gǎnmào le?

B：Kěnéng shì. Zuótiān búshì xià yǔ le ma? Wǒ méi dài sǎn, bèi yǔ lín le.

A：Nà wǒmen qù kàn yíxià yīshēng ba?

B：Xiān búyòng le, wǒ xiǎng xiān shuì yīhuìr, shuì xǐng kěnéng jiù hǎo le.

A：Xíng ba, nǐ xiān xiūxi.Xiàwǔ rúguǒ hái bù shūfu, wǒmen jiù qù kàn yīshēng.

B：Hǎo de, bù hǎoyìsi, jīntiān bùnéng qù bówù guǎn le.

A：Méi guānxi, shēntǐ yàojǐn !

 内练习 Exercises

一 **分角色朗读课文**。Role-play the conversation.

二 **根据课文内容，回答问题**。Answer questions according to the text.

    1. 他们今天要去哪儿?

    2. B怎么了?

    3. B为什么会感冒?

    4. B想去医院吗?

    5. 他们今天还去博物馆吗?

三 **听一听，跟读句子**。Listen and read the sentences.

    1. 我有点儿不舒服，头有点儿疼。

    2. 我没带伞，被雨淋了。

    3. 我们去看一下医生吧?

    4. 下午如果还不舒服，我们就去看医生。

    5. 没关系，身体要紧!

生词学习 New words

舒服（形）	shūfu	comfortable
头（名）	tóu	head
疼（形）	téng	painful
感冒（动）	gǎnmào	get a cold
伞（名）	sǎn	umbrella
淋（动）	lín	drench
医生（名）	yīshēng	doctor

不用（副）	búyòng	need not
醒（动）	xǐng	wake
休息（动）	xiūxi	rest
身体（名）	shēntǐ	body

 课文 Texts

课文二

A：早上好，医生。

B：早上好，哪儿不舒服？

A：我头疼，嗓子疼，可能还有点儿发烧。

B：那先测一下体温吧。三十八点五度，是有点儿烧。

这样多久了？

A：我昨天被雨淋了，晚上开始有点头疼，

今天早上嗓子也开始疼了。

B：服用过什么药没有？

A：没有。医生，我的病严重吗？

B：不要紧，就是普通感冒。

A：那我要怎么办呢？

B：我给你开点儿药。

回去以后，要多喝水，多休息休息。

如果三天以后还没退烧就再来医院看一下。

A：好的，谢谢医生。

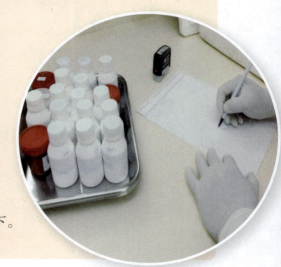

kèwén èr

A：Zǎoshàng hǎo, yīshēng.

B：Zǎoshàng hǎo, nǎr bù shūfu?

A：Wǒ tóu téng, sǎngzi téng, kěnéng hái yǒudiǎnr fāshāo.

B：Nà xiān cè yíxià tǐwēn ba. Sānshíbā diǎn wǔ dù, shì yǒudiǎnr shāo.

Zhèyàng duō jiǔ le?

A：Wǒ zuótiān bèi yǔ lín le, wǎnshàng kāishǐ yǒudiǎnr tóu téng,

　　jīntiān zǎoshàng sǎngzi yě kāishǐ téng le.

B：Fúyòngguo shénme yào méiyǒu?

A：Méiyǒu. Yīshēng,wǒ de bìng yánzhòng ma?

B：Bú yàojǐn, jiùshì pǔtōng gǎnmào.

A：Nà wǒ yào zěnmebàn ne?

B：Wǒ gěi nǐ kāi diǎnr yào.

　　Huíqù yǐhòu, yào duō hē shuǐ, duō xiūxi xiūxi.

　　Rúguǒ sān tiān yǐhòu hái méi tuìshāo jiù zài lái yīyuàn kàn yíxià.

A：Hǎo de, Xièxie yīshēng.

课内练习 Exercises

一　**分角色朗读课文**。Role-play the conversation.

二　**根据课文内容，回答问题**。Answer questions according to the text.

1. 这个对话发生在哪里？

2. A 哪里不舒服？

3. A 发烧了吗？

4. A 吃过药吗？

5. 医生让 A 做什么？

三　**听一听，跟读句子**。Listen and read the sentences.

1. 哪儿不舒服？

2. 我头疼，嗓子疼，可能还有点儿发烧。

3. 先测一下体温吧。

4. 要多喝水，多休息休息。

5. 如果三天以后还没退烧就再来医院看一下。

生词学习 New words

嗓子（名）	sǎngzi	throat
发烧（动）	fāshāo	have a fever
测（动）	cè	measure
体温（名）	tǐwēn	body temperature
度（名）	dù	degree
烧（名）	shāo	fever
服用（动）	fúyòng	take (medicine)
药（名）	yào	medicine
病（名）	bìng	illness
严重（形）	yánzhòng	serious
普通（形）	pǔtōng	normal
开（药）（动）	kāi（yào）	prescribe (medicine)
退（烧）（动）	tuì（shāo）	reduce (a fever)

语言点链接 Language points

一 "还"的用法 Usage of "还（hái）"

副词"还"表示某个动作或状态的持续，否定形式常用"还没"。

Adverb "还" means a continuation of an action or a situation. The negative form is often expressed as "还没"。

（1）你怎么还没起床?

（2）十点了，他还在睡觉。

（3）我们的旅行还没结束。

（4）我们还在中国旅行。

二 反问句"不是……吗"的用法 Usage of the rhetorical question "不是……吗"

反问句"不是……吗"主要用来表达说话者的强烈的语气或者态度，经常表示惊讶、不理解、不满意或者责备等。

The rhetorical question "不是……吗" is mainly used to express the speaker's strong tone or attitude, often indicating surprise, confusion, dissatisfaction, or reproach.

（1）你怎么还没起床？我们今天不是说好去博物馆的吗？

（2）A：我想吃比萨。

　　　 B：我们不是刚吃完晚饭吗？

（3）你不是去北京了吗？怎么还在这里？

（4）不是说今天会下雨吗？怎么没下？

三 "多+v."的用法Usage of "多（duō）+v."

"多+v."表示在原来的基础上有所增加，常常用来劝说更多地去做某件事情。

"多+v." indicates an increase from the original and is often used to encourage someone to do more of a certain activity.

（1）多喝水，多休息休息。

（2）你可以多听听汉语歌曲。

（3）你要多听多说，才能学好汉语。

四 "如果……就……"的用法Usage of "如果（rúguǒ）……就（jiù）"

"如果……就……"用来表示假设，有时候"如果"可以不说。

" 如 果 …… 就 ……" is used to indicate a supposition, meaning "if, in case". Sometimes "如果" can be omitted.

（1）如果明天天气好，我们就去爬长城。

（2）如果明天我身体好了，我们就去故宫。

（3）如果你喜欢，我就多买一些。

（4）如果你没时间，明天我就一个人去吧。

五 "v.+过"的用法Usage of "v.+过（guò）"

"v.+过"可以表示某个已经发生的动作或者状态，用来强调过去有过的某种经历。

"v.+过" can indicate an action or state that has occurred, and is used to emphasize a certain experience in the past.

S	P		
	v.	过	O
他	来	过	中国。
我	去	过	这家公司。
我	吃	过	中国菜。

它的否定形式是在动词前面加"没（有）"。

Its negative form is to add "没（有）" before the verb.

S	P		
	没（有）+v.	过	O
他	没（有）来	过	中国。
我	没（有）去	过	这家公司。
我	没（有）吃	过	中国菜。

它的疑问形式是在句末加"没有"。

Its interrogative form is to add "没有" at the end of the sentence.

S	P		
	v.	过	O+ 没有
你	服用	过	药没有？
他	来	过	中国没有？
你	去	过	这家公司没有？
你	吃	过	中国菜没有？

六 "被"字句的用法 Usage of "被（bèi）sentence"

"被"字句是指在核心动词前面，用介词"被（给、叫、让）"引出施事或单用"被"的表示被动的主谓句。被字句的基本结构为"S+被+n.+v.+other elements"。当"被"字句用来强调结果的时候，施事者可以省略。

"被 sentence" refers to a subject predicate sentence that uses the preposition "被（给、叫、让）" before the main verb to introduce the agent or simply uses "被" to indicate the passive voice. The basic structure is "S+被+n.+v.+other elements". When it is used to emphasize the result, the agent of the action can be omitted.

S（Receiver）	被	n.（agent）	v.	other elements
我	被	雨	淋	了。
电脑	被	我	弄	坏了。
我的行李	被	—	偷	了。
小偷	被	—	抓	住了。

"被"字句的否定要在"被"前加"没"，并且句末没有"了"。

The negative form is to add "没" before "被" and there's no "了" at the end of the sentence.

S（Receiver）	adv.	被	n.（agent）	v.	other elements
我	没	被	雨	淋	。
电脑	没	被	我	弄	坏。
我的行李	没	被	—	偷	。
小偷	没	被	—	抓	住。

课后练习　Exercises

一 **看拼音写汉字**。Look at the pinyin and write the words.

bó wù guǎn　　shū fu　　tóu téng　　yào jǐn　　xiū xi

（　　　）　（　　　）　（　　　）　（　　　）　（　　　）

fā shāo　　fú yòng　　yán zhòng　　pǔ tōng　　rú guǒ

（　　　）　（　　　）　（　　　）　（　　　）　（　　　）

二 **改写句子**。Rewrite the sentences.

1. 例如：他来过中国。

　　　　　他来过中国没有？

　　　　　他没（有）来过中国。

（1）我已经去过长城了。

_____

（2）我在中国旅游过。

_____

（3）去年我们去上海迪士尼玩过。

_____

（4）我吃过很多中国菜。

_____

（5）我看过这部电影。

_____

2. 例如：我把门关上了。

　　　　门被（我）关上了。

　　　　门没被关上。

（1）小狗把花瓶打碎了。

_____

（2）我把衣服弄脏了。

_____

（3）我把车撞坏了。

_____

（4）我把手机落在出租车里了。

_____

（5）风把我的帽子吹走了。

_____

三 **替换画线部分**。Replace the underline parts with the given words or phrases.

1. 你怎么还没起床？

①你怎么／没吃饭　　　　②下周我／在上海　　　③我／没结束旅行

_____

2. 昨天不是下雨了吗？

①他的生日／明天　　　　②我们／刚去过上海　　③眼镜／就在桌子上

_____

3. 生病了，你要多喝水。

①病好了以后／可以去运动运动

②去中国以后／可以去几个地方玩

③有时间的话／可以在中国待几天

_____

4. 如果还不舒服，我们就去看医生。

①下午不下雨／我们／出发去上海

②你有不懂的／你／来问我

③你不忙／我们／现在出发

_____

四 把下面的词语整理成句子。Rearrange the following words and phrases to make sentences.

1. 我们　不是　今天　去　打篮球　说好　吗

2. 如果　还　下午　我们　就　下雨　了　不去　超市

3. 我　偷　昨天　手表　的　被　了

4. 医生　我　一点儿　药　开　了　给

5. 不是　昨天　了　下雨　吗

五 听录音，判断对错。Listen to the recording and judge whether the statements are correct or incorrect.

1. 男生到医院来看朋友。　　　　　☐

2. 男生头疼，发烧了。　　　　　　☐

3. 男生是昨天半夜开始不舒服的。　☐

4. 男生昨天喝酒了。　　　　　　　☐

5. 医生让男生回去以后多喝酒。　　☐

旅游小贴士 Travel Tips

如何在中国医院就诊？

在一个陌生的国家生病是一件不愉快的事情。但是如果你在中国旅行的时候真的生病了，你知道如何在中国就医吗？

首先，在中国有公立医院和私立医院之分。小型的私人诊所很少。

其次，你需要知道中国的医疗急救电话是120。你可以在任何你觉得有需要的时候拨打120，救护车会很快赶来。

当然大部分时候我们都可以自行前往医院就医。就医的时候请记得带上您的护照。

1. 挂号

您可以提前通过医院热线或者网上预约挂号，也可以到医院后在医院的挂号窗口进行挂号。挂号的时候您需要提交您的护照进行登记并支付一定金额的挂号费，之后您会拿到一张病历卡。

2. 就诊

挂号完之后您就可以去医生办公室等待就诊了。医生办公室外面有签到机，您需要先签到一下，然后在诊室外等候叫号就诊。

就诊时医生可能会根据您的情况需要安排进一步的仪器检查。他会给你开检查单，您需要在支付相关检查费用之后到专门的检查中心去进行进一步的检查。

3. 复诊

做完检查之后，请您耐心等候检查结果。通常大部分检查结果会在1—2个小时左右出来。结果出来后，您需要回到接诊医生的诊室继续就诊。

4. 开药

病情不严重的情况下，医生会给您开出处方，您在收费处进行缴费之后直接在医院的药房领取您的药。医院的药房通常都在医院一楼大厅中。

5. 住院

如果您的病情需要住院或者手术，医生在确认是否还有床位或者是否有条件手术后，会给您安排住院手续。当然您会需要预缴一些费用。

How to seek medical treatment in China?

It is never a pleasant experience to fall sick or ill in an unfamiliar country. However, if you fall ill while traveling in China, here's how to navigate medical care:

First, the Chinese medical system comprises mostly of public and private hospitals. Small and personalized clinics are very uncommon.

The first thing you should know about local medical services is the emergency call number 120. You can dial 120 whenever you need it. An ambulance will usually arrive very quickly.

Of course, most of the time we may go to the hospital for medical treatment ourselves. Please remember to bring your passport with you when seeking medical treatment.

1. Register

You can make an appointment in advance by calling the hospital hotline or booking online. Alternatively, you can register at the hospital's registration window. You will need to present your passport, register, and pay a registration fee. Afterward, you will receive a medical record card.

2. Diagnosie

After registering, you can go to the doctor's office and wait for a doctor's treatment. There is a check-in machine outside the doctor's office where you need to sign in before waiting outside the consultation room for your number to be called.

The doctor may order additional tests based on your condition. You will receive a test order form, and you need to pay for the tests before going to the designated testing center for further examination.

3. Return visit

After completing the examination, please be patient and wait for the results. Usually, most of the examination results will be available within 1-2 hours. After the results come out, you need to go back to the doctor's office for a follow-up consultation.

4. Prescribe medicine

In cases where the condition is not severe, the doctor will provide you with a prescription, and you will make the payment at the cashier and directly collect your medicine from the hospital pharmacy, usually located in the lobby on the first floor of the hospital.

5. Hospitalize

If your condition requires hospitalization or surgery, the doctor will check for available beds or necessary conditions for surgery and arrange the admission procedures. Of course, you will need to pay a deposit for hospitalization.

附录

Appendix

 课文翻译

第一单元　机场

第一课　登机

Text one

A: I'd like to buy a plane ticket to Shanghai.

B: Are you looking for a one-way ticket or a round-trip ticket?

A: Round-trip ticket.

B: Which day? May I ask when you plan to depart?

A: I'll depart tomorrow and return next Tuesday.

B: Would you prefer economy class or business class?

A: Economy class.

B: Here's your ticket.

A: Okay, thank you.

Text Two

A: Excuse me, is this where I check in for the flight to Shanghai?

B: Yes, it is. What kind of seat would you like, window or aisle?

A: Window, please.

B: Alright, do you have any luggage to check in?

A: Yes. Here is my suitcase.

B: Okay. There's no problem with the luggage. Here is your boarding pass and luggage claim ticket. You may proceed to security now.

A: Thank you.

第二课　机上服务

Text One

A: Welcome aboard this flight. Please fasten your seatbelt, as our plane is about to take off. Hello, is there anything I can help you with?

B: I'm feeling a bit cold. Could I have a blanket, please?

A: Of course, sir. Let me adjust the air conditioning for you first.

B: Thank you.

A: Sir, here's the blanket you requested.

B: Thank you.

Text Two

A: Hello, sir. What would you like to drink?

B: What do you have?

A: We have apple juice, orange juice, pineapple juice, coffee, tea, and water.

B: I'll have a glass of apple juice, please.

A: Certainly, sir. Here's the in-flight meal we provide. Enjoy your meal.

B: Thank you.

(Before landing)

A: Ladies and gentlemen, our aircraft is about to land. Please adjust your seatbacks, open your window shades, and fasten your seatbelts. Thank you for your cooperation.

第三课　出境

Text One

A: Hello, may I see your valid identification, please?

B: Hello. Here is my passport.

A: Thank you. Could you please remove your hat? I appreciate your cooperation. What brings you to China?

B: I'm here to study Chinese.

A: How long do you plan to stay in China?

B: One year.

A: Alright, I wish you a successful study.

Text Two

A: Hello, is this Mss. Zhang?

B: Yes, is this Shadi?

A: Yes, it's me. I have passed through customs. Now I am waiting for my luggage.

B: Alright, I'll wait for you at the exit. Don't worry.

A: Thank you. Mss. Zhang, thank you for coming to the airport to pick me up. I appreciate it.

B: Don't mention it. You must be tired after the journey. The airport transportation is very convenient，we can take the subway to the school.

A: That's great. Let's go.

第二单元　交通

第四课　出租车

Text One

A: Hello, where would you like to go?

B: Hello, I'd like to go to the Kaiyuan Hotel.

A: Alright.

B: How long does it take to drive from the airport to the hotel？

A: If there's no traffic, it's about 40 minutes away.

B: That's quite far.

A: Although it's a bit far, the hotel is very nice.

B: Really? I'm looking forward to it.

Text Two

A: Hello, we've arrived at the hotel.

B: How much is it in total?

A: It's a total of 80 yuan. You can scan the QR code to pay.

B: I'm sorry, can I pay with cash?

A: No problem.

B: Alright, here's 80 yuan for you.

A: Don't forget your luggage.

B: Thank you, goodbye!

A: Goodbye!

第五课　地铁

Text One

A: Hello, I'd like to visit the Tianyi Pavilion. Which subway line should I take?

B: You can take Subway Line one and get off at the Ximenkou Station.

A: Okay, how do I buy a ticket?

B: You can buy a ticket at the ticket vending machine.

A: Sorry, it's my first time in Ningbo, could you teach me?

B: First select your destination station, then choose the number of tickets, and finally pay.

A: Okay, thank you very much.

B: You're welcome.

Text Two

A: Hello, your bag needs to go through a security check.

B: Alright.

A: Is there a bottle of water in your bag?

B: Yes, It's a bottle of mineral water I just bought.

A: Since some dangerous liquids are not allowed on the subway, it is required to take a sip to verify it.

B: Okay, no problem.

A: Thank you for your cooperation.

第六课　高铁

Text One

A: I'd like to travel to Hangzhou.

B: Great, how should we get there?

A: I think the high-speed train is quite convenient.

B: How do we buy tickets?

A: We can buy tickets using our phones or go to the ticket window.

(At the high-speed rail ticket counter)

A: Hello, I'd like to buy high-speed rail tickets to Hangzhou.

C: Alright, are you leaving today?

A: Yes.

C: What time would you like to leave?

A: Are there any tickets for around 10 o'clock?

C: Wait a moment, let me check for you. How about the high-speed rail departing at 10:45?

A: That's fine, I'll take two tickets. Here are our passports.

C: That'll be a total of 142 yuan.

Text Two

A: We will arrive in Hangzhou in just an hour!

B: China's high-speed rail can reach speeds of up to 350 km/h. The speed of China's high-speed rail is faster than ours.

A: Yes, China's high-speed rail is fast and safe.

B: I heard we can even order takeout.

A: Really? China's high-speed rail service is getting better and better.

B: Next time we can try it.

A: Good idea!

第三单元　酒店

第七课　入住

Text One

A: Hello, is this Kaiyuan Hotel? I would like to book a room.

B: May I ask if you are the only one? When would you like to check-in?

A: Check in on May 10th and check out on May 12th.

B: Just a moment, I'll check if there are any rooms available. There is another room left.

A: How much is the room fee? Does it include breakfast?

B: A room costs 500 yuan, including breakfast. Breakfast is served from 7 to 9 o'clock.

A: Okay, please reserve that room for me.

B: Please confirm. May 10th to 12th, one single room.

A: That's right.

Text Two

A: Hello, Kaiyuan Hotel. How can I help you?

B: Hello, I would like to check in.

A: Do you have a reservation?

B: I have reserved a single room.

A: Okay, could you please show me your passport?

B: Can you arrange a room on a higher floor?

A: No problem, please wait a moment. This is the room card. Your room number is 1007, on the tenth floor.

B: Okay, thank you.

A: If you need any further services, please contact the front desk. Wishing you a pleasant stay.

第八课　酒店服务

Text One

A: Excuse me, where can I dine?

B: The restaurant is on the sixth floor. However, you can also call for a meal and a server will deliver it to your room.

A: That's great! Do you also offer wake-up call services?

B: Yes, you can call 1236 and tell the front desk what time you need to wake up.

A: By the way, is there WiFi in the room?

B: Yes, the password is eight 8s.

A: One more thing, where can I exchange for RMB?

B: Turn right outside the hotel and there is a bank.

A: Okay. Thank you.

Text Two

A: Good evening, Reception. May I help you?

B: I left my room card in the room.

A: Can you tell me your room number?

B: Room 1007.

A: May I ask your name?

B: My name is Shadi.

A: Okay, we'll send staff over immediately to help you open the door.

B: Thank you.

A: You're welcome. Feel free to contact us if you have any questions.

第九课　退房

Text One

A: Hello, I'd like to check out of room 1007.

B: Okay, please give me your room card.

A: Here, how much do I need to pay?

B: The waiter is checking the room. Could you please wait a moment? Is there any charge in the room?

A: No.

B: Sorry for keeping you waiting. Please confirm, two nights, a total of 980 yuan, either in cash or by scanning the QR code.

A: Paid. By the way, could you please call a car for me? I need to go to the airport.

B: No problem, please wait a moment and I will call a car for you right away

Text Two

A: Hello, I'm checking out of room 1007. What is the check-out time?

B: At 12 o'clock, please check out in advance.

A: Okay, I would like to temporarily store my luggage. Is there any extra charge?

B: No. Guest luggage storage is free.

A: That's great.

B: Are you satisfied with our hotel's service?

A: The room is quite nice, it would be better if the bed were a little softer.

B: Thank you for your suggestion. We will work on improving it next time.

第四单元　活动

第十课　银行

Text One

A: Hello, what service do you need?

B: Hello, I need to withdraw 1,000 dollars in cash.

A: Yes, have you made an appointment?

B: Yes, I made an appointment last week.

A: Okay, please enter your password.

B: Let me think about it.

A: Sorry, the password is not correct, please enter it again.

B: What about this one?

A: This is correct. Please wait a moment.

B: Okay, thank you.

Text Two

A: Hello, what service do you need?

B: Hello, I want to get a transaction statement

A: Yes, you can do it right here on this machine.

B: Can you help me with that?

A: Sure, you can select the time frame here.

B: I need the statement for the past three months.

A: OK, just press the "Confirm" button here.

B: Thank you, it's much easier to handle these things now than before.

第十一课　餐厅

Text One

A: Welcome! Here's our menu.

B: Okay, do you have any recommendations?

A: Our Sauteed Bamboo Shoots are very popular here.

B: Okay, let's try it.

A: From your accent, it sounds like you're from the north?

B: Yes, I haven't tried this dish before.

A: You should give it a try.

B: Okay, let's order this one.

Text Two

A: Ah, I'm starving. Let's order quickly.

B: Okay. Do you eat spicy food?

A: Mild spice is fine.

B: How about Mapo Tofu?

A: It's a bit too spicy for me.

B: How about Stir-fried Beef with Green Peppers?

A: Great. I like beef a lot.

B: Ha ha, me too. Let's also get some scrambled eggs with tomatoes.

第十二课　商店

Text One

A: It's a nice dress, what do you think?

B: It's nice, but I'd like to buy some special souvenirs.

A: What do you want to buy?

B: I'd like to buy some local handicrafts, such as traditional embroidery or porcelain.

A: Let's go to a handicraft store nearby.

B: Okay, let's go and have a look.

A: There's a nice store here. They have lots of local specialties.

B: Great!

Text Two

C: Hello, welcome! What do you need?

A: We would like to see what local specialties you have in your store.

C: Of course, we have a lot of traditional handicrafts here.

B: This tea set looks exquisite, you can take it as a souvenir.

C: Yes, this tea set is handmade with great care and attention to every detail.

A: Alright, we'll take this tea set.

C: Great, this tea set is 298 yuan, do you need to pay by credit card or cash?

B: Let's do it by credit card.

C: Okay. Thank you for your visit and have a nice trip!

B: Thank you and good luck with your business!

第五单元　应急

第十三课　迷路

Text One

A: Excuse me. I got lost. Can you tell me how to get to this place?

B: Let me see. Are you going to the museum here?

A: Yes, yes. Can you tell me how to get there?

B: I'm heading in that direction, too. Let me take you there!

A: Thank you so much! Is this place far away from the museum?

B: Not far. It'll be a ten-minute walk.

B: Here, the museum is right next to the bank. You can cross the road. I'll go first.

A: Thank you so much ! Goodbye!

Text Two

A: Excuse me. Can you tell me where I am on the map?

B: Let me see, we are here. Where are you going?

A: I may be lost. I want to go to the train station. How can I get to the train station from here?

B: Let me think about it. You can take the subway to the train station. Take Line 1 to the Gulou first, and then transfer to Line 2 to the railway station.

A: Thank you so much! Where can I take the subway?

B: Walk along the road to the intersection, then turn right, keep going straight, and you can see the subway station.

A: Great, thank you.

B: you're welcome ! Goodbye!

第十四课　物品遗失

Text One

A: Hello, Sir! What can I help you?

B: Hello, I can't find my luggage.

A: Don't worry. How many pieces of luggage did you lose?

B: Just one piece. I was having coffee in the cafe and put my luggage under the table. After I finished my coffee, the suitcase was gone.

A: What does your lost suitcase look like?

B: It's a very small brown leather suitcase with my name sticker on it.

A: Maybe someone took it by mistake. Please leave your name and contact information with me, and we will try our best to find it for you.

B: Okay, how long will it take?

A: I'm sorry. I don't know right now. What about this: you can head back, and we will inform you as soon as we have any news?

B: Okay, thank you.

Text Two

A: Hello, what can I help you?

B: Hello, I came to pick up my lost suitcase .

A: Ok, please have a seat first. Can you please show me your ID card?

B: Of course, here you are.

A: Thank you, please tell me what your suitcase looks like.

B: A small brown suitcase, with my name posted on it.

A: Ok, I'm sure it's your suitcase. You can take it away.

B: You've been very responsible and very warm-hearted. Thank you!

A: You're welcome!

第十五课　就医

Text One

A: Shadi, why aren't you up yet? Didn't we agree to go to the museum today?

B: I'm not feeling well. My head hurts a little.

A: Are you catching a cold?

B: Maybe. It rained yesterday. I didn't bring an umbrella and got soaked.

A: How about seeing a doctor?

B: Not yet, I want to sleep for a while. I may feel better ok after the rest.

A: All right, have a rest first. If you're still feeling not good in the afternoon, we will see the doctor.

B: Okay, sorry we can't go to the museum today.

A: It doesn't matter. Health is the most important.

Text Two

A: Good morning, doctor.

B: Good morning. What's the matter?

A: I have a headache, a sore throat, and probably a little fever.

B: Take your temperature first... Thirty-eight and five degrees, there is a little fever. How long has this been going on?

A: I was caught in the rain yesterday. I began to have a headache at night, and my throat began to hurt this morning.

B: Have you ever taken any medicine?

A: Not yet. Doctor, is my illness serious?

B: Never mind, just a common cold.

A: What should I do?

B: I'll give you some medicine. When you get home, drink plenty of water and get lots of rest. If the fever has not gone down after three days, come to the hospital again.

A: Ok, thank you, doctor.

课后练习答案

第一单元　机场

第一课　登机

一、看拼音写汉字。Look at the pinyin and write the words.

zhí jī	ān jiǎn	guò dào	xiǎng	jī piào
（值机）	（安检）	（过道）	（想）	（机票）

hái shi	chū fā	dān chéng	jīng jì cāng	xíng li
（还是）	（出发）	（单程）	（经济舱）	（行李）

二、选词填空。Choose the correct word to fill in the blanks.

1. 我（想要）喝咖啡。
2. 请问是在这里（值机）吗？
3. 请问你买（经济舱）还是商务舱？
4. 这张机票是去（上海）的。
5. 你想这周（还是）下周去拜访别的公司？

三、把下面的词语整理成句子。Rearrange the following words and phrases to make sentences.

1. 你想要面包还是牛奶？／你想要牛奶还是面包？
2. 请问我们哪天出发？
3. 她想买一张电影票。
4. 这是你的行李箱吗？
5. 我们下周去上海。

四、回答问题。Answer the qestions.

略。

五、听录音，判断对错。Listen to the recording and judge whether the statements are correct or incorrect .

1. F　2. F　3. T　4. F　5. T

第二课　机上服务

一、看拼音写汉字。Look at the pinyin and write the words.

huān yíng	háng bān	qǐ fēi	kōng tiáo	tǎn zi
（欢迎）	（航班）	（起飞）	（空调）	（毯子）

tí gōng	jí jiāng	jiàng luò	diào zhí	pèi hé
（提供）	（即将）	（降落）	（调职）	（配合）

二、选词填空。Choose the correct word to fill in the blanks.

1. 请（给）我一杯苹果汁。
2. 您想要喝（咖啡）还是茶？
3. 您可以（帮）我调直椅背吗？
4. 请您（配合）我们的安检。
5. 我们的飞机还有半个小时就要（起飞）了。

三、把下面的词语整理成句子。Rearrange the following words and phrases to make sentences.

1. 她要放假了。
2. 我帮他搬家。／他帮我搬家。
3. 请您系好安全带。
4. 祝您用餐愉快。
5. 我们的飞机即将降落。

四、回答问题。Answer the qestions.

略。

五、听录音，判断对错。Listen to the recording and judge whether the statements are correct or incorrect.

1. F　2. F　3. F　4. F　5. T

第三课　出境

一、看拼音写汉字。Look at the pinyin and write the words.

zhèng jiàn	mào zi	dǎ suàn	zhù	shùn lì
（证件）	（帽子）	（打算）	（住）	（顺利）

tōng guò	chū kǒu	jiāo tōng	fāng biàn	dì tiě
（通过）	（出口）	（交通）	（方便）	（地铁）

二、选词填空。Choose the correct word to fill in the blanks.

1. 祝你工作（顺利）。

2. 我们现在（出发）去上海。

3. 谢谢您的（配合）。

4. 你还要（多长时间）可以到学校？

5. 我正在回答（海关人员）的问题。

三、把下面的词语整理成句子。Rearrange the following words and phrases to make sentences.

1. 我们几点出发？

2. 今天太热了。

3. 他已经到了。

4. 这里的地铁很方便。

5. 我在这里等你。／你在这里等我。

四、回答问题。Answer the qestions.

略。

五、听录音，判断对错。Listen to the recording and judge whether the statements are correct or incorrect.

1. F　2. F　3. T　4. T　5. T

第二单元　交通

第四课　出租车

一、看拼音写汉字。Look at the pinyin and write the words.

èr wéi mǎ	xiàn jīn	zuǒyòu	sǎo miáo	yígòng
（二维码）	（现金）	（左右）	（扫描）	（一共）

qī dài	jiǔ diàn	dǔ chē	kě néng	yǒudiǎnr
（期待）	（酒店）	（堵车）	（可能）	（有点儿）

二、选词填空。Choose the correct word to fill in the blanks.

1. 不要（忘记）带护照。

2. 这个地方很（不错）。

3. 请问您怎么（付钱）？

4. 他非常（期待）这次见面。

5. 北京有三个（机场）。

三、对话配对。Match the sentences.

　　1-C　2-E　3-D　4-A　5-B

四、把下面的词语整理成句子。Rearrange the following words and phrases to make sentences.

　　1. 今天有点儿热。

　　2. 你吃了吗？

　　3. 她可能是中国人。

　　4. 开车需要 30 分钟。

　　5. 他能写汉字。

五、听录音，判断对错。Listen to the recording and judge whether the statements are correct or incorrect .

　　1. T　2. T　3. T　4. F　5. T

第五课　地铁

一、看拼音写汉字。Look at the pinyin and write the words.

méi wèn tí	pèi hé	xū yào	xuǎn zé	ān jiǎn
（没问题）	（配合）	（需要）	（选择）	（安检）

cān guān	fēi cháng	chéng zuò	xià chē	yì píng shuǐ
（参观）	（非常）	（乘坐）	（下车）	（一瓶水）

二、选词填空。Choose the correct word to fill in the blanks.

　　1. 您好，欢迎（乘坐）本次航班。

　　2. 买票的时候（需要）出示你的护照。

　　3.（因为）今天天气不好，所以我们决定去图书馆。

　　4. 我想去北京的故宫（参观）。

　　5.（怎么）去上海呢？

三、句子配对。Match the sentences.

　　1-B　2-E　3-A　4-C　5-D

四、把下面的词语整理成句子。Rearrange the following words and phrases to make sentences.

　　1. 你听听这首歌曲。

2．你是不是想去北京？

3．请问票怎么买？

4．他想去图书馆看书。

5．你可以学习学习汉语。

五、听录音，判断对错。Listen to the recording and judge whether the statements are correct or incorrect .

1．F　2．F　3．F　4．F　5．T

第六课　高铁

一、看拼音写汉字。Look at the pinyin and write the words.

hǎo zhǔ yi	lǚ yóu	huò zhě	jué de	shāo děng
（好主意）	（旅游）	（或者）	（觉得）	（稍等）

fú wù	xiǎo shí	ān quán	tīng shuō	gāo tiě
（服务）	（小时）	（安全）	（听说）	（高铁）

二、选词填空。Choose the correct word to fill in the blanks.

1．这里乘坐高铁很（方便）。

2．他想买一部（手机）。

3．这辆车的（速度）很快。

4．你觉得这家饭店的（服务）怎么样？

5．他们什么时候（出发）？

三、句子配对。Match the sentences.

1-C　2-A　3-B　4-E　5-D

四、把下面的词语整理成句子。Rearrange the following words and phrases to make sentences.

1．我觉得今天挺热的。

2．还有十分钟就下课了。

3．我们的衣服比他们的便宜。

4．这里的水果又新鲜又便宜。

5．这个地方越来越漂亮了。

五、听录音，判断对错。Listen to the recording and judge whether the statements are correct or incorrect .

1．T　2．F　3．T　4．T　5．T

第三单元　酒店

第七课　入住

一、看拼音写汉字。Look at the pinyin and write the words.

jiǔ diàn	yù dìng	rù zhù	què rèn
（酒店）	（预订）	（入住）	（确认）

kè rén	gōng sī	tí qián	yā jīn
（客人）	（公司）	（提前）	（押金）

二、选词填空。Choose the correct word to fill in the blanks.

1．请稍等，我帮您（查）一下。

2．（房间）里的空调坏了，可以来修一下吗？

3．请你（为）我们换一些人民币。

4．我的行程有变，我需要（取消）预订机票。

5．我打算 3 号（入住），7 号退房。

三、替换画线部分。Replace the underline parts with the given words or phrases.

略。

四、把下面的词语整理成句子。Rearrange the following words and phrases to make sentences.

1．我想预订一个双人间。

2．我帮你检查检查吧。/你帮我检查检查吧。

3．你什么时候回来？

4．晚餐时间从 6 点到 8 点半。

5．我要看一下护照。

五、听录音，判断对错。Listen to the recording and judge whether the statements are correct or incorrect.

1．F　　2．T　　3．T　　4．F　　5．T

第八课　酒店服务

一、看拼音写汉字。Look at the pinyin and write the words.

kě yǐ	shùn biàn	qǐ chuáng	cān tīng	diàn huà
（可以）	（顺便）	（起床）	（餐厅）	（电话）

hào mǎ	mǎ shàng	wèn tí	suí shí	gōng zuò
（号码）	（马上）	（问题）	（随时）	（工作）

二、选词填空。Choose the correct word to fill in the blanks.

1. 直走，然后往左（拐），银行就在你的右边。

2. 我喜欢大（一点儿）的房间。

3. （可以）帮我个忙吗？

4. 这次我们（派）你代表我们参加。

5. 可以给我（换）个房间吗？

三、对话配对。Match the sentences.

1-E 2-A 3-D 4-C 5-B

四、把下面的词语整理成句子。Rearrange the following words and phrases to make sentences.

1. 这件衣服太大了。

2. 酒店旁边有一个银行。／银行旁边有一个酒店。

3. 可以帮我打扫一下房间吗？

4. 你找到护照了吗？

5. 健身房在酒店一楼。

五、听录音，判断对错。Listen to the recording and judge whether the statements are correct or incorrect.

1. T 2. T 3. F 4. T 5. F

第九课　退房

一、看拼音写汉字。Look at the pinyin and write the words.

duō shǎo	huò zhě	xiāo fèi	jī chǎng	yí gòng
（多少）	（或者）	（消费）	（机场）	（一共）
tí qián	bàn lǐ	shōu fèi	mǎn yì	yào shi
（提前）	（办理）	（收费）	（满意）	（钥匙）

二、选词填空。Choose the correct word to fill in the blanks.

1. 今天（或者）明天都行，只要你能来。

2. 这里停车（收费）吗？

3. 如果你不能入住，请（提前）取消预约。

4. 这次你们派了（多少）人参加比赛？

5.（要是）明天他不来，那我们就取消会议。

三、替换画线部分。Replace the underline parts with the given words or phrases.

略。

四、把下面的词语整理成句子。Rearrange the following words and phrases to make sentences.

1. 这次来了多少人？

2. 我给妈妈买花。/ 妈妈给我买花。

3. 行程已经安排好了。

4. 他对房间很满意。

5. 他在看书呢。

五、听录音，判断对错。Listen to the recording and judge whether the statements are correct or incorrect.

1. F　2. T　3. F　4. T　5. T

第四单元　活动

第十课　银行

一、看拼音写汉字。Look at the pinyin and write the words.

xiàn jīn	mì mǎ	yè wù	shū rù	bàn lǐ
（现金）	（密码）	（业务）	（输入）	（办理）

què dìng	cāo zuò	liú shuǐ	fàn wéi	xuǎn zé
（确定）	（操作）	（流水）	（范围）	（选择）

二、选词填空。Choose the correct word to fill in the blanks.

1. 我护照（呢）？刚刚还在包里的。

2. 你（再）尝尝，现在味道怎么样？

3. 这个商场（近）吗？

4. 导游（让）我们在这里等她。

5. 我已经说三（遍）了！

三、对话配对。Match the sentences.

1-D　2-C　3-E　4-B　5-A

四、把下面的词语整理成句子。Rearrange the following words and phrases to make sentences.

1．我预约了今天取现金。

2．在机器上操作太方便了。

3．我想看看这张卡的银行流水。

五、听录音，判断对错。Listen to the recording and judge whether the statements are correct or incorrect．

1．T 2．F 3．F

第十一课 餐厅

一、看拼音写汉字。Look at the pinyin and write the words.

huān yíng guāng lín	kǒu qì	běi fāng	diǎn cài	
（欢迎光临）	（口气）	（北方）	（点菜）	
gǎn jǐn	xǐ huan	cài dān	tuī jiàn	cān tīng
（赶紧）	（喜欢）	（菜单）	（推荐）	（餐厅）

二、选词填空。Choose the correct word to fill in the blanks.

1．听你的（口气），刚来中国吗？

2．尝尝（看），味道怎么样？

3．这个餐厅很受（欢迎）。

4．游客很（喜欢）在这里拍照。

5．谁（点）的菜？太辣了！

三、对话配对。Match the sentences.

1．D 2．A 3．B 4．E 5．C

四、填写正确的菜肴名。Fill in the correct dish name.

A.青椒牛柳 B.麻婆豆腐 C.油焖笋 D.番茄炒鸡蛋

五、听录音，判断对错。Listen to the recording and judge whether the statements are correct or incorrect．

1．T 2．T 3．F

第十二课　购物

一、看拼音写汉字。Look at the pinyin and write the words.

dāng dì	huò zhě	fù jìn	tè sè	chǎn pǐn
（当地）	（或者）	（附近）	（特色）	（产品）

dàng zuò	shǒu gōng	zhì zuò	xì jié	lǚ tú
（当作）	（手工）	（制作）	（细节）	（旅途）

二、选词填空。Fill in the blanks with words .

1．这家餐厅的菜品不仅美味，而且摆盘非常（精美）。

2．她每天都会（用心）准备自己的工作。

3．我们一家人在海边度过了一个（愉快）的假期。

4．祝您的生意（兴隆），越来越红火。

5．这家酒店采用（传统）的建筑风格，非常有特色。

三、对话配对。Match the sentences.

1-E　2-C　3-D　4-A　5-B

四、填写正确的补语完成句子。Fill in the correct complement to complete the sentence.

1．你的新衣服看（起来）很漂亮。

2．这本书可以带（进去）吗？

3．走（过去）的那个人是你朋友吗？

4．这个菜看（起来）不怎么样，吃（起来）很不错啊！

5．我妈说我买（回来）的东西很用心。

五、听录音,判断对错。 Listen to the recording and judge whether the statements are correct or incorrect .

1. F　2. F　3. F

第五单元　应急

第十三课　迷路

一、看拼音写汉字。Look at the pinyin and write the words.

mí lù	gào su	zǒu lù	páng biān	lù kǒu
（迷路）	（告诉）	（走路）	（旁边）	（路口）

zhuǎn	kàn jiàn	dì fang	mǎ lù	bó wù guǎn
（转）	（看见）	（地方）	（马路）	（博物馆）

二、选词填空。Choose the correct word to fill in the blank.

1. 我今天先不去了，明天（再）去。

2. 我好像（迷路）了，还没找到博物馆。

3. 去博物馆需要（换乘）地铁。

4. （往）左走 100 米就到博物馆了。

5. 我今天有点累。因为（一直）在走路。

三、改写句子。Rewrite the sentences.

1. 爸爸让我帮他修一下电脑。

2. 检票员让她出示她的护照。

3. 姐姐让我跟她一起去上海。

4. 妈妈让我赶紧去洗澡。

四、替换画线部分。Replace the underline parts with the given words or phrases.

略。

五、把下面的词语整理成句子。Rearrange the following words and phrases to make sentences.

1. 您能告诉我怎么去医院吗？

2. 让我带您过去吧。

3. 医院就在学校左边。／学校就在医院左边。

4. 沿着这条路往前走。

5. 您可以坐地铁去机场。

六、听录音，判断对错。Listen to the recording and judge whether the statements are correct or incorrect

1. T　2. F　3. T　4. T　5. F

第十四课　物品遗失

一、看拼音写汉字。Look at the pinyin and write the words.

xíng li	zháo jí	lián xì	jǐn liàng	tōng zhī
（行李）	（着急）	（联系）	（尽量）	（通知）
diū shī	gāng cái	fù zé	rè xīn	bāng zhù
（丢失）	（刚才）	（负责）	（热心）	（帮助）

二、选词填空。**Choose the correct word to fill in the blanks.**

1. 今天太晚了，你（别）走了。

2. 请把这张海报（贴）到墙上。

3. 听说他昨天把手机（丢）了。

4. 老师给我们（留）了很多作业。

5. 最近我们都很忙，我（尽量）在周五完成这个项目。

三、改写句子。**Rewrite the sentences.**

1. 你看得见海报上的字吗？
   我看不见海报上的字。

2. 你听得懂中国人说话吗？
   我听不懂中国人说话。

3. 你听得清楚我说的话吗？
   我听不清楚你说的话。

4. 他今天做得完作业吗？
   他今天做不完作业。

四、替换画线部分。**Replace the underline parts with the given words or phrases.**
略。

五、把下面的词语整理成句子。**Rearrange the following words and phrases to make sentences.**

1. 我来取之前丢失的手机。

2. 我找不到我的手机了。

3. 请您一有消息就通知我。

4. 您把姓名和电话留给我。／您把电话和姓名留给我。

5. 上面写着起飞的时间。

六、听录音，判断对错。**Listen to the recording and judge whether the statements are correct or incorrect**

1. F　2. T　3. F　4. F　5. T

第十五课　就医

一、看拼音写汉字。**Look at the pinyin and write the words.**

bó wù guǎn	shū fu	tóu téng	yào jǐn	xiūxi
（博物馆）	（舒服）	（头疼）	（要紧）	（休息）

fā shāo	fú yòng	yán zhòng	pǔ tōng	rú guǒ
（发烧）	（服用）	（严重）	（普通）	（如果）

二、改写句子。Rewrite a sentence

1.（1）你去过长城没有？

   我没（有）去过长城。

（2）你在中国旅游过没有？

   我没（有）在中国旅游过。

（3）去年你们去上海迪士尼玩过没有？

   去年我们没（有）去上海迪士尼玩过。

（4）你吃过中国菜没有？

   我没（有）吃过中国菜。

（5）你看过这部电影没有？

   我没（有）看过这部电影。

2.（1）花瓶被打碎了。

   花瓶没被打碎。

（2）衣服被弄脏了。

   衣服没被弄脏。

（3）车被撞坏了。

   车没被撞坏。

（4）手机被落在出租车里了。

   手机没被落在出租车里。

（5）我的帽子被吹走了。

   我的帽子没被吹走。

三、替换画线部分。Replace the underline parts with the given words or phrases.

略。

四、把下面的词语整理成句子。Rearrange the following words and phrases to make sentences.

1．我们不是今天说好今天去打篮球吗？

2．如果下午还下雨，我们就不去超市了。

3．昨天我的手表被偷了。

4．医生给我开了一点儿药。

5．昨天不是下雨了吗？

五、听录音，判断对错。Listen to the recording and judge whether the statements are correct or incorrect.

1. F　2. F　3. T　4. T　5. F

听力文本

第一单元　机场

第一课　登机

A：您好，我想买一张去广州的机票。

B：好的，什么时候？

A：今天还有机票吗？

B：有的，今天下午。

A：好的，我买两张。

B：您想买经济舱还是商务舱？

A：我买两张经济舱。

B：好的，您需要靠窗的位置还是靠过道的位置？

A：靠过道的。

B：您要买往返票吗？

A：不，谢谢。

B：好的，这是您的机票。请您今天下午一点到机场办理值机。

A：好的。谢谢。

第二课　机上服务

A：您好，我们的飞机将在半小时后起飞，请您系好安全带。

B：您好，可以帮我调直椅背吗？

A：好的，先生。还有什么需要帮助的吗？

B：我有点儿热。

A：好的，我帮您调大风量。

B：请问有冰水吗？

A：有的，稍等。这是您要的冰水。

B：谢谢。

A：先生，您要牛肉饭还是鸡肉饭。

B：牛肉饭。

A：祝您用餐愉快。

B：谢谢。

第三课　出境

A：你通过海关了吗？

B：我已经通过海关了。

A：顺利吗？

B：顺利。工作人员问我来干什么，我告诉他我是学生。

A：你现在在做什么？

B：我在等我的行李。

A：好的，我在三号出口等你。

B：谢谢你来机场接我。

A：不客气。我们一会儿坐地铁去学校。

B：好的。

第二单元　交通

第四课　出租车

1. A：老师，你能说英语吗？

   B：当然可以。

   A：老师，你能说法语吗？

   B：不好意思，我不会法语。

   A：我可以教你。

   B：真的吗？我很期待。

2. A：您好！请问这本英语书多少钱？

   B：60块。

   A：那这本汉语书呢？

   B：50块。

   A：我都要，请问一共多少钱？。

   B：110块。

3．A：机场在哪里？

B：机场在东边。

A：离这家饭店远吗？

B：开车需要 50 分钟左右。

A：有点儿远啊。

B：是的，我们要早点出发。

4．A：您好，我们到了。

B：有点儿快啊。

A：一共是 20 块。

B：我可以用现金吗？

A：当然可以，您也可以扫描二维码付钱。

B：我用现金吧。

5．A：您好，我要去开元度假村。

B：好的，度假村里面有酒店和饭店，您是去哪一个？

A：我要去酒店。

B：好的，酒店有点儿远。需要 30 分钟左右。

A：好的，没问题。

第五课　地铁

1．A：你好，请问怎么去鼓楼？

B：你可以坐地铁或者乘坐出租车。

A：地铁站离这里远吗？

B：不远，就在前面。

A：好的，谢谢。

B：不客气。

2．A：您好！您的包需要安检。

B：好的。

A：您的包里是不是有几瓶水？

B：是的。

A：这些水需要您试喝一口。

B：没问题。

3. A：我们一起去北京吧。

B：好啊，我们怎么去呢？

A：我们可以坐飞机去。

B：你知道北京哪里好玩吗？

A：当然，我已经去过一次了。

B：太好了。

4. A：我们去买地铁票吧。

B：可是我不会用购票机。

A：没关系，我会用。

B：真的吗？那我要看看怎么买票。

A：没问题，我可以教教你。

5. A：听说中国菜很好吃。

B：真的吗？我们去尝尝吧。

A：我们先去吃饺子，然后去吃年糕。

B：好啊，我们去哪里吃？

A：我们可以找一家中国饭店试试。

第六课　高铁

1. A：你周末准备去哪里？

B：我还没想好，你呢？

A：我想去爬山。

B：爬山？那里风景怎么样？

A：我觉得很漂亮。

B：那我们一起去吧。

2. A：你会游泳吗？

B：当然。

A：你小时候就会游泳吗？

B：是的，我五岁就会了。

A：你很厉害，是谁教你的？

B：我的妈妈。

3. A：你们在聊什么？又说又笑的？

B：我们在聊昨天的电影。

A：我没看，那部电影怎么样？

B：非常精彩，我们都很喜欢。

A：真的吗？我也要去看。

4．A：刚刚那个人是你弟弟吗？

B：不是，是我朋友。

A：你今年十八岁对吗？

B：是的

A：那你朋友呢？

B：我朋友二十岁。

5．A：你刚才是在用中文聊天吗？

B：是的，我现会用中文跟中国人聊天了。

A：你来中国多长时间了？

B：快一年了。

A：你的汉语进步很大

B：真的吗，谢谢！

第三单元　酒店

第七课　入住

客人：你好，我想入住酒店。

前台：好的，请问您预订了房间吗？

客人：是的，我预订了一间双人房。

前台：请问您的预订姓名是？

客人：我的预订姓名是张三。

前台：好的，让我来查一下。是的，我们已经为您预订了一间双人房，您需要填写登记表并提供有效的身份证明。

客人：好的，这是我的护照。

前台：谢谢，我帮您登记一下。您的房间号是303，电梯在右手边，请您注意。

客人：好的，谢谢。

前台：另外，我们提供免费早餐，早餐时间是早上6点到10点，您可以在一楼的餐厅享用。

客人：好的，谢谢。

前台：不客气，祝您入住愉快。

客人：谢谢。

第八课　酒店服务

客人：你好，我想问一下，您们提供叫车服务吗？

前台：是的，我们有专门的叫车服务。请问您需要什么时间的车？去哪里？

客人：我想在明天晚上 7 点叫一辆去机场的车。

前台：好的，我来帮您安排。请问您需要帮忙预订机票吗？

客人：需要，顺便帮我们预订托运行李服务。

前台：好的，请问您需要哪个航班的机票，有几件行李需要托运？

客人：我需要预订明天晚上 7 点的 MU256 航班，行李有两件。

前台：好的，让我来帮您预订机票和行李托运。请您提供身份证明，以便我们为您
　　　办理手续。

客人：好的，这是我的护照。

前台：好的，谢谢。请您稍等片刻，我会尽快为您安排。

客人：好的，谢谢。

前台：另外，请问您需要我们帮忙叫醒服务吗？

客人：需要，请在明天早上 6 点叫醒我。

前台：好的，我来帮您安排。请问您还有其他需求吗？

客人：暂时没有了，谢谢。

前台：不客气，祝您旅途愉快。

第九课　退房

客人：你好，我想退房。

前台：好的，您的房间号码是多少？

客人：我的房间号码是 202。

前台：好的，让我来检查一下。好的，您的账单已结清。请问您对我们的服务满
　　　意吗？

客人：是的，非常感谢。我在这里住得很愉快。

前台：太好了，我们很高兴听到这个好消息。您需要我们帮您叫出租车吗？

客人：是的，请帮我叫一辆出租车去机场。

前台：好的，我会帮您安排好的。谢谢您的入住，祝您旅途愉快。

客人：谢谢您。再见！

前台：再见！

旅游汉语

第四单元　活动

第十课　银行

　　我是一名大三学生，目前正在银行实习。今天我碰到了一位母亲，她来银行拉流水，她说她女儿准备出国，需要国内有足够的资金证明。我帮助她在银行自助机上拉了半年的流水，操作很方便，她很满意。

第十一课　餐厅

　　上周三我和朋友小李去了一家小饭馆吃晚饭。这家饭馆离我们很远，我们开了近一小时的车，但对我们来说，这家饭馆的菜太辣了。

第十二课　商店

　　我的俄罗斯朋友很喜欢喝茶，对她来说，去一个地方旅游，最好的纪念品就是那个地方的茶。所以她生日的时候，我送了她一套精美的茶具。

第五单元　应急

第十三课　迷路

A: 请问，这儿离机场远吗？

B: 有点儿远。

A: 那你能告诉我怎么去机场吗？

B: 你可以坐机场大巴，也可以坐地铁。

A: 我应该坐几号线呢？

B: 你可以先坐 3 号线然后换乘 4 号线

A: 附近有地铁站吗？

B: 就在前面。你往前走到路口往右转就能看到地铁站了。

A: 非常感谢！

B: 不客气。

第十四课　物品遗失

A: 您好，女士！有什么可以帮您？

B: 您好，我在你们店里丢了手机，你们可以帮我找一下吗？

A: 您别担心，先想一下，手机可能在哪里丢的？

B: 我中午在你们的餐厅吃饭。吃饭的时候我把手机放在桌子上。吃完饭后我还用手机支付了。出去打车的时候发现手机找不到了。

A: 您丢的是怎么样的手机?

B: 是一个华为手机，黑色的，背面套着一个紫色的手机壳。

A: 请您稍等，我帮您找一下。

B: 好的，谢谢您。

（5分钟后）

A: 女士，您好，我们有找到一个手机，您看一下是不是您的?

B: 是的，就是我的，太感谢你们了。

A: 不用谢，这是我们应该做的。

第十五课　就医

A: 您好，医生!

B: 你好，哪儿不舒服?

A: 我拉肚子了。

B: 什么时候开始的?

A: 昨天半夜的时候开始不舒服。

B: 昨天吃了什么?

A: 也没什么。晚上和朋友一起去吃烧烤了，还喝了几瓶啤酒。

B: 你先去抽个血，化验一下。

（半个小时后）

A: 医生，怎么样，我没事吧?

B: 我看了报告了，有点肠胃炎，问题不大。

A: 那我要怎么办呢?

B: 我给你开点儿药。回去以后，要多喝水，多休息休息，少喝酒。

A: 好的，谢谢医生。